PLEASURE GROUNDS

PLEASURE GROUNDS

The Gardens and Landscapes of Hampshire
edited by
Gill Hedley and Adrian Rance,
Southampton City Art Gallery and Museums
with a foreword by
Sir Hugh Casson, CH, KCVO, PPRA, RDI, RIBA

Published by Milestone Publications on the occasion
of the exhibition *Pleasure Grounds*
held at Southampton City Art Gallery, 1987,
in conjunction with
The Hampshire Gardens Trust

Published by
Milestone Publications
62 Murray Road,
Horndean, Hampshire PO8 9JL

Design Sue Hudson
Edited by Gill Hedley and Adrian Rance

Typeset by The Monitor, Hayling Island, Hampshire
Printed and bound in Great Britain by
R.J. Acford, Industrial Estate, Chichester, Sussex

Pleasure grounds : the gardens and landscapes
   of Hampshire.
   1. Landscape gardening——England——
   Hampshire——History
   I. Hedley, Gill
712.6′09422′7   SB466.G75H3

ISBN 1-85265-104-0

Foreword

SIR HUGH CASSON
CH, KCVO, PPRA, RDI, RIBA

As one who greatly enjoys gardens but is reluctant to labour in them — (I once threatened to pave the family window box) — I am not perhaps the obvious choice to introduce a book on the gardens and landscape of Hampshire. But, as one who has lived on and off in this beautiful county for over fifty years, I am well aware of the pressures for development, private and public, that threaten what is left of our open spaces.

Much of this development is of course sensible and necessary. . . just as refusal to accept any changes can be infantile, (particularly as so often it achieves a small good at the expense of a larger one). What is needed is a wider and more knowledgeable awareness of the history and value of our local landscape heritage, and more encouragement of and help to owners — public and private — to look after their treasures, old and new. We need to identify priorities, to promote conservation studies and, above all, to cultivate in each one of us a sharper eye for landscape and a sense of affection and responsibility for its delights.

These are some of the admirable aims of the Hampshire Gardens Trust. They are set out and celebrated in the Pleasure Grounds Exhibition (Southampton Art Gallery, May 23rd - June 28th) and in the pages of this illustrated book.

We are grateful to all those who have helped — (financially or otherwise) — in organising this splendid project that draws attention to the conflicting problems ahead and guides us towards imaginative and sensible solutions.

The authors and publishers wish to thank the following who have kindly provided photographic illustrations for this book.

Heather Angel

Mavis Batey

Bodleian Library

The British Architectural Association : Drawings Collection

The Trustees of The British Museum

Broadlands (Romsey) Ltd.

Paul Carter, Viewpoint

Courtauld Institute of Art

Fitzwilliam Museum, Cambridge

Hampshire County Council

Hampshire County Museums Service

Hampshire Record Office

Lucinda Lambton

Eric Lane

Joyce Moore

Portsmouth City Museums

Royal Botanic Gardens, Kew

The Royal Commission on the Historic Monuments of England

The Scolar Press

The Gilbert White Museum, Selborne

Sotheby's

Dr Nigel Temple

Winchester City Museums

The Yale Center for British Art

The Hampshire Gardens Trust

The Hampshire Gardens Trust was founded in 1984, in response to the need to provide a means of caring for the county's outstanding gardens and landscapes. An ongoing survey records both vanishing landscapes and opportunities for conservation.

Gardens can be works of art, or of special historic interest, or they may be of horticultural, architectural, scientific or scenic importance. Above all, gardens give pleasure and refreshment; they are of value to the community.

The aim of the Trust is to stimulate interest in gardens, enthusiasm for their care and an appreciation of their value. We work with owners, advising and encouraging them to make use of the professional conservation skills available from government agencies, local authorities, professional consultants and voluntary organisations. We work with schools and have an educational programme called "Learning Through Landscapes." We provide opportunities for members of the public to learn about the history of the design and development of gardens and to become involved in conservation.

The purpose of this book and of the exhibition, "Pleasure Grounds. The Gardens and Landscapes of Hampshire," is to enable us to look at our gardens with new eyes, to see more than just the beauties of the plants themselves.

We are deeply grateful to Sir Hugh Casson, to those who have contributed this fascinating series of essays, to the editors Gill Hedley and Adrian Rance, to the designer, Sue Hudson, and to the publisher, Nicholas Pine of Milestone Publications.

We hope you will support the work of the Hampshire Gardens Trust and help us to care for our pleasure grounds.

Mrs. MALDWIN DRUMMOND
Chairman

This book commemorates the achievement of the gardeners and those who enjoy gardens in Hampshire. It is a permanent record of the exhibition, "Pleasure Grounds. The Gardens and Landscapes of Hampshire," generously sponsored by Wensley Hayden-Baillie in memory of his family who lived at Bramshill House for two hundred and thirty-nine years, and by Hampshire County Council and The Countryside Commission.

Contents

Above:
Paul Sandby, *Hackwood*, Yale Center for British Art

Left:
Paul Sandby, *Hackwood*, The British Museum

PLEASURE GROUNDS
The Gardens & Landscapes of Hampshire

GILL HEDLEY
KRYSTYNA BILIKOWSKI

Hampshire is a county of downland, forest, heathland, coastline, great houses, cottages, market towns and industrial cities. The appearance of its landscape is often man-made, altered for agricultural or industrial needs, but we are concerned here with the design of its public spaces, its private estates, city parks and gardens of all sizes. Although there might have been other considerations in their layout the landscapes and gardens discussed here can be unified as pleasure grounds, designed for beauty and enjoyment.

On the whole our knowledge of early gardens in the county is confined to documentary references and illustrations in paintings, drawings, plans or prints and in the next chapter Dr. Landsberg describes the process of recreating gardens in Winchester, Southampton and Petersfield.

The Bishop of Winchester's Pipe Roles from 1208 onwards gives many references to his deer park at Highclere. Records of William of Wykeham's residence at Highclere exist for every year between 1368 and 1384, 1392 and 1394, and 1398. Many of the entries relate to the enclosure or mending of the park boundary, the planting of trees for timber within the park or to stocking the park with deer. There are entries recording the construction of the fish ponds within the park which were later naturalised by 'Capability' Brown, as Milford Lake, in the 1770's.

The references to the gardens at Highclere show that they were typical of their period. There were fruit gardens and herb gardens; in 1367 four carpenters were hired for a day to raise and support the palisade about the herb garden which had been blown down by the wind. In 1400 there are accounts for a carpenter making a new 'mentellum and capellum by which the Lord may go into the garden'. It took four days to make and cost 16d; it was lathed and tiled. This was probably a sheltered gallery by which Bishop Wykeham could walk into the garden.

The fullest accounts of a monastic kitchen garden are from Beaulieu in the 13th century. There, one official was in charge of several gardens: kitchen and herb and pleasure gardens. Onions and cereals were grown and there are entries in the accounts for herb seeds, gloves, sieves and gravels as well as the mending of garden spades, forks and buckets. Honey and cider were produced from their own hives and orchard.

The 16th century saw an expansion of large, private mansions and Basing House was one of the most beautiful and well known. Queen Elizabeth was entertained there on several occasions by her Treasurer Sir William Paulet, who had been Henry VIII's Comptroller. In 1531 Sir William obtained permission to rebuild the medieval stronghold of the St. John family within the Norman ringwork of Basing. The first house which he built at Basing was greatly influenced by Hampton Court: built in brick it had a gatehouse and courtyards; the garden walls which still survive are inset with two pigeon houses. In 1539 he became Lord St. John. 20 years later during the years of the Protectorate Government after Henry VIII's death, he became one of the wealthiest men in the country and built an 'New House at Basing'. There was a grander gatehouse than that of the 1530's and a new axis gave a different line of approach. A banqueting house at Basing was placed at the upper end of the rampart terrace and was backed by a triangular shaped orchard[1]. Contemporary with his building of the New House at Basing he was building a London residence, Winchester House at London Wall. Queen Elizabeth visited Basing several times and although there is no description, as there is for her visit to Elvetham in 1591, she would have been entertained with similar pageants and banquets.

The landscaping of Elvetham, the summer residence of the Seymour family, was on a grand and theatrical scale. Edward Seymour organised a masque to entertain the Queen on her visit to his house in 1591. Apart from massive building work to the house, Seymour constructed an open air setting for the entertainment and had a pond built "cut to the perfect figure of a half moon". In the pond was a 'ship isle', 100ft × 40ft, with 'three trees orderley set out for three masts', a 'fort' 20ft square and 'overgrown with willows' and a 'snayl mount rising to four circles of green privie hedge 20ft high and 40ft broad at the bottom'.

In contrast to this dramatic and now vanished landscape is Bramshill built by Lord Zouche in the 17th century to a carefully planned design. Little is known of the original design but a 'troco' or area for bowls remains. Medieval features can still be seen and Maze Hill remains as the only record of its maze. A lake, a sconce-shaped (fort-like) island, a series of walled gardens, an ornamental postern gateway and octagonal turrets on the gateway survive, probably from Lord Zouche's design. He was a member of a circle of highly educated and illustrious botanists and horticulturalists, which included the famous John Tradescant.

Despite the Civil War siege laying waste to Basing House and its gardens, the site was to continue in some importance. Its walled gardens were used for growing fruit and Cecila Fiennes on her visit in 1690 records the gardens as much improved with new walls, fine woods and vineyards. The Paulet family transferred their seat to nearby Hackwood and Charles Paulet built there, in 1688, a large house on the site of the hunting lodge. Hackwood had been part of the extensive deer park of Basing Castle and the new house at Hackwood was linked to Basing with long avenues. During the 18th century, as the picturesque attitude to ruins grew with a corresponding antiquarian interest, the ruins of Basing House were landscaped and a picturesque lodge was built overlooking the orchard and Tudor gardens. It is not clear who was responsible for this work but it may have been Charles Paulet, grandson of the third Duke of Bolton and Lavinia Fenton, his second Duchess.

At Hackwood, the formal French style gardens were set out about 1720 probably by the architect James Gibbs, in the style of Le Notre. There are eight formal avenues radiating from a 'rond point' and the wood is surrounded on three sides by raised earthwork terraces. A survey of 1807 by William Brown shows the formal landscape, much of which is replaced by later landscaping. An 'Intended Water Piece' was dug and still exists but was never completed. The earthwork terraces of the amphitheatre remain as does a cockpit. The original woodland character of the 18th century Spring Wood has been replaced by exotic Victorian planting.

West Green House sits in a formal landscape on the 1773 Tylney Hall estate map which shows that an obelisk was part of the 18th century layout. There is also a formal 'sconce-shaped' entrance forecourt clearly visible. The house was the home of General Henry Hawley and either he or his adopted son Captain William Toovey-Hawley was responsible for laying out

1. Unpublished report by Mavis Batey, Garden History Society.

the grounds. Although adapted as a garden feature throughout the 17th and 18th centuries this defensive feature may have been consciously used in the design at West Green House due to its military, defensive associations.

During the 18th century, the cultural education of noblemen included a Grand Tour to Italy and Greece to develop a taste for classical sculpture and antiquities. A portrait by Angelica Kaufmann at Broadlands shows Henry, second Viscount Palmerston, holding a plan for the temple at Paestum alluding to the influence that classical taste had on wealthy patrons. The taste for the antique was widespread:

> "The English countryside swarmed with English parsons whose love of antiques was often their most sincere profession. . . by 1762 the English public was more curious about antiques than ever before'.[2]

The gardens of Hampshire shelter many classical curiosities. At Hurstbourne a Graeco-Roman torso has been reclothed to represent George III as a Roman Emperor. 'Jackdaws Castle' at Highclere incorporates six classical columns from Berkeley House in London, and is an eye catcher in the form of a classical temple at the end of a vista. A wooden Tuscan temple also used to punctuate the scene.

Some fragments of Netley Abbey were re-erected in the grounds of Cranbury Park in the 1760's in keeping with the picturesque taste for ruins. In Gilpin's words:

> 'A pile gains from a state of ruin, an irregularity in its parts . . . which the eye examines with renewed delight'.[3]

Follies, grottos and hermitages were also created as amusements for the eye and intellect. The Lisle sisters (nine of them) at Crux Easton constructed a grotto of which nothing remains but Alexander Pope's commemorative lines:

> "Here shunning idleness at once and praise,
> This radiant pile nine rural sisters raise
> The Glittering emblem of each spotless dame,
> Pure as her soul and shining as her fame
> Beauty which nature only can impart,
> And such polish as disgraces art;
> But fate dispos'd them in this humble sort,
> And held in deserts what could charm a court".

Robert Herbert at Highclere constructed several follies which survived 'Capability' Brown's improvements and Hackwood's Spring Wood was interspersed with follies. Several designs survive at Hackwood for buildings, either projected or built, by Vardy and Lord Bolton himself.

A grotto still exists at Walhampton and one is pictured on an estate map of 1787. This has been attributed to the Boatswain of Admiral Sir Harry Burrard Neale (1768-1840)[4]. It is described as being made of tufa with a log pediment, arched door and an iron grille. However, it is just as likely that the construction could have been of twig work in the rustic style as later summer houses at Mottisfont Abbey and Stratfield Saye. Today the grotto is set in a 10ft square brick garden house which is later in date and may have been part of the redesign of the gardens by Thomas Mawson in 1913. The maps shows a mount surrounded by a low hedge and planted with low shrubs. A little blue (timber?) pavilion or summerhouse sits on the top. This was probably on top of the mount which still lies between Portmore Pond and Sandwalk Pond. The canal and Sandwalk Pond seem to have been made more serpentine in form, the shape of Sandwalk Pond being

2. Lipking, Lawrence *The Ordering of the Arts in Eighteenth Century England*, Princeton, 1970, p. 141.

3. Gilpin, William, *Observation on several parts of the counties of Cambridge, Norfolk, Suffolk and Essex, etc.*, 1809, p. 121-2.

4. Jones, Barbara *Follies and Grottoes*, Constable, 1974.

comparable with the shape of many fish ponds, notably those pre-dating the construction of Milford Lake in Highclere Park. The 1787 map shows in general a formal landscape with many features which, by this date, could be considered unfashionable. However, these may belong to an earlier layout. Also shown is a formal canal, later naturalised in shape, a mount, and two formal avenues one stretching northwards towards Vicars Hill, Boldre, where the Reverend William Gilpin lived and the other, southwards into the pleasure grounds.

The Orangery, Broadlands

Lancelot 'Capability' Brown dominates most histories of English landscape design but does not dominate Hampshire to quite the same degree. This is due in part to the disappearance of many of the great houses for which he worked: Warnford, Cuffnells and Paultons have all been lost. His influence, however, was wide ranging and his pupils, Richard Woods and William Eames, worked in the county. Eames worked at Dogmersfield, Brockenhurst and possibly at Cuffnells and Elvetham while Woods is known to have worked at Old Alresford House.

The Brownian landscape with its natural curves, serpentine lakes, clumps of trees and sweeping lawns was an important stimulus. Commissioned by the nobility to modernise and drastically to alter their large estates, his 'natural' style often inspired other landowners to look carefully at their own grounds and find in them the 'capability' for improvement.

Brown's earliest work in Hampshire was in 1764 at Broadlands for the second Viscount Palmerston. The first Viscount had been responsible, before his death in 1757, for 'giving away all the fine pyramid greens to those who will fetch them of which many cart loads have gone already'.[5] thus destroying the scene described by Cecilia Fiennes in the 1680's (see page 73). The second Viscount asked Brown to design the landscape and Henry Holland to re-model the house (in partnership with his father-in-law, Brown). Brown created a sweeping, grassy slope down to the river which itself was widened in front of the house.

Throughout the next decade, Brown worked on several estates including a large commission at Highclere for Henry Herbert, later the Earl of Carnarvon. After an initial visit by Brown, a longer visit was made by John Spyers who produced full surveys of both the grounds and the house. From these, Brown made his own large plan which was submitted to Henry Herbert. This large plan was composed of three sections and closely resembles in style the plan for Boarn Hill Cottage. At Highclere, the work of implementing the designs was undertaken by the estate workers, under Mr. Herbert's instruction. Brown's improvements were superimposed on the earlier rococo park. Characteristically, Brown banished the detail and colour of the flower, fruit and kitchen gardens to a hidden, walled enclosure. The major elements of Brown's design at Highclere follow his broad method of landscape design with a 'natural' landscape using clumps and bolts of trees, with water introduced as an integral feature and drives leading out around the perimeter of the park.

On 11 December 1775, Brown stayed with Lord Bute and wrote to his wife:

> 'I stay'd with Lord Bute two nights and each Day we drank a bottle of Toca(y) wine which was rather too much for me as my cough has been troublesome'.[6]

They would have discussed Lord Bute's plans for Highcliffe, above Christchurch Bay (now in Dorset), a site chosen by Bute when he left office as Prime Minister in 1762 and was devoting much time to his study of rare plants. The extent of building work undertaken at Highcliffe is uncertain but a 'bathing place' was attributed to "Capability" Brown. Gilpin mentions that Lord Bute had attempted a clifftop plantation and the gardens at Highcliffe contained many of the rare plants found in the neighbourhood. Lord Bute subsequently published a nine volume work on the different species of British flora.

In 1776, Brown was also involved in the design of a marine villa by Henry Holland for Robert Drummond, Brown's own banker. Drummond's estate was at Cadland on Southampton Water but extending to the Solent shore. There in 1780, Holland designed a cottage orné known first as Boarn Hill, used for outings and fishing trips from the main house. This part of the Solent shore was mainly scrub oak and Brown planted extensively using evergreen oak, beech, sweet chestnut and Scots pine. He provided a circuit walk with contrasting moods and succeeded in suggesting a far larger scale that its eight acres. Brown's inscription to his plan mentions 'the Sea Bank Path of Gravel amongst the Firs, Bushes. . . a Path or Walk under the Hedge with Shrubs & Plants that will Grow'.

5. Stroud, Dorothy *Capability Brown.*
6. *op. cit.*

Brown later wrote to Drummond:

'On looking over the Accts. I find you added for my trouble on the Out of Doors work, £200, which is more than I can possibly accept of from you, by £100, I having a reasonable profit in the Building'.[7]

Cadland is also notable for the only known application by a hermit to take up residence on an estate and provide his own design for a hermitage (see p. 59).

Besides Highcliffe and Cadland there are other marine villas in the county which were set out in designed grounds in the 1780's and 1790's. In Hamble, Sir John Soane built Sydney Villa between 1789 and 1798, with grounds sloping down to the Solent. At Exbury, the Mitford family had a country house set in a small park, with a garden mount, as at Walhampton, giving scenic seaside views. This house and parkland form the base upon which the Rothschilds were to develop their world famous collection of rhododendrons in the 1920's and 30's (see p.25). The seaside climate offered a temperate microclimate suitable for the growing of tender and exotic trees and shrubs. John Plaw, a Southampton architect, known for his books of designs for country houses and rustic curiosities mentions the:

'Ground Plan of a design made for a situation near Titchfield. The front towards the south commanding a very extensive sea view towards the east and west, from St. Helen's point to the Needles; directly opposite is the Isle of Wight'.

Plaw's *Ferme Ornée or Rural Improvements* of 1795 includes designs for John Morant of Brockenhurst Park who commissioned Eames and Webb to design his estate in 1793. The design for a hunting gate incorporates the letter M to be painted 'of a colour different from the gate and give a general idea of the hunt to which they belong: they also show the extent of the proprietor's domain'. Plaw also designed a fishing lodge and keeper's dwelling which was 'intended to have been executed with roots and trunks of trees, near the river in his park'. It incorporated accommodation for tea drinking parties and fishing tackle with lodgings for the keeper and his family behind. Plaw also designed a Bath House supplied with hot and cold water (sufficient to make a full tepid bath; there are provisions also for a shower bath occasionally) but unfortunately, these designs do not seem to have been executed due to John Morant's untimely death in 1794.

Picturesque estate cottages, in general, replaced the gothic ruins and classical temples as objects of interest to be placed in the landscape. A superb example of the cottage orné style translated into a house for the owner himself is Houghton Lodge built before 1801 on a beautiful site on the Test. It is in the gothic style and John Nash has often been suggested as its architect. Lawns were raised so that the house commands the view and the grounds are planted with exotic trees. House and site combine to produce a picturesque effect enhanced by the rustic flint grotto used as an archway, over the original drive.

Picturesque estate villages were created at Rotherfield and Hursley and painted by G.F. Prosser in the 1830's and 40's.

In 1800, Stratton Park was sold by Francis Russell, Duke of Bedford, to Sir Francis Baring. He immediately set about 'improving' his estate. Baring commissioned Humphry Repton in 1801 to produce a design for building a new house in a landscape setting.

Repton set out to establish himself as the successor to 'Capability' Brown and succeeded in securing himself the position of the leading landscape

7. Cadland House, Drummond Archives.

John Griffier, *Hurstbourn Priors,*
English Heritage

Humphry Repton, *Stratton Park Red Book*,
Private Collection

gardener (a term he coined himself) in England. He was aware that his own style of design did differ in many ways from that of Brown and his followers, such as Eames or Woods, but he continued to defend his predecessor's reputation. However, Repton was much more concerned with the 'character' of the estates which he was called in to redesign and although his work is less grand than Brown's it is also less ruthless, and more sympathetic. If 'capability' was the word most associated with Brown, 'variety' is that which best describes a Repton park. He is remembered also for his charming Red Books which contained delicate watercolours with an overlaid sheet, which, when flat, showed the 'before' and unimproved scene and, when lifted, showed the transformation. Between illustrations were

Jane Pars, *Rotherfield with an artist sketching*, Private Collection

the text containing the conversations between designer and client as they walked around the park planning its improvement. The Red Book for Stratton Park survives. Repton's proposal for a new house were not accepted, probably for financial reasons, and it has generally been thought that his landscape proposals were also ignored. However, it can be seen that Baring did act upon a number of Repton's suggestions. The park was extended eastwards and it appears that the turnpike road on the western edge of the park was moved to its present position in 1833. Repton believed that the main problem affecting the park was the intrusion of noise from this road.

In 1806, Baring commissioned George Dance to draw up plans for improving the existing house. Dance's drawings are in the Soane Museum and include plans for nine pairs of cottages. These estate cottages are planned entirely symmetrically, each with its own garden. The plans also include designs for lodges at the main London and Winchester entrances. Dance's design including the house, were accepted and East Stratton was developed into a rustic and picturesque estate village as it remains today.

Repton also undertook work at Herriard House, near Basingstoke in 1793 and Norman Court, Stockbridge, about 1807-10. Neither Red Book survives.

J.C. Buckler, *North-West View of Bramshill*, Private Collection

Repton's youngest son George Stanley Repton also worked in Hampshire. Between 1832 and 1833 he refronted the outer court of the Warden's lodgings at Winchester College and worked on the New Commons there between 1837 and 1839 and the Headmaster's house between 1839 and 1841. He designed a porch for Hursley Park in 1834 and altered the church tower there in the same year. He designed Shirley Rectory in 1839 and in the 1840's designed a conservatory for F.L. Beckford at his house in Southampton.[8]

Repton began to work more on suburban villas than on great estates in his later career and he made use of the increasing number of rare plants imported from abroad by plant collectors. Botany and horticulture were important scientific and intellectual disciplines; many notable scholars and practitioners lived and worked in Hampshire. John Worlidge wrote his *Systema Horticulturae or the Art of Gardening*, in 1667, in Petersfield. John Goodyer, a distinguished 17th century botanist, also lived in Petersfield. William Curtis was born in Alton in 1746 and, after practising as an apothecary in London, established a botanical garden there in 1771 and published his *Flora Londinensis* in 1775 ('a new and original Botanic Work, intended to comprehend all the Plants which grow wild in Great Britain, beginning first with those which are found *in the environs of London*').

In 1779, he opened a 'London Botanic Garden' in Lambeth and in 1787 began to publish *The Botanical Magazine*, now usually referred to as *Curtis's Botanical Magazine*. Fourteen volumes were issued until his death in 1799 and the magazine still continues to be published, now as *The Kew Magazine*. Its sub-title was 'The Flower-Garden Displayed' and its coloured plates and descriptive text are both decorative.

Curtis was a founder member of the Linnaean Society in 1778 and, the

8. Carter, Goode & Laurie, *Humphry Repton Landscape Gardener*, Sainsbury Centre for Visual Arts, 1982, pp. 134 & 153.

next year saw his Botanic Garden established at Brompton, with greenhouses, a library and subscription catalogue.

Sir George Leonard Staunton, the Irish diplomat and plant collector, was on Lord MaCartney's embassy to China between 1792 and 1794. Staunton was particularly interested in botany and the embassy was instrumental in collecting and recording plants unknown in England at the time.

Also on the embassy was Staunton's twelve year old son George Thomas whose education included the study of botany. Later when George Thomas Staunton was employed by the Honourable East India Company, from 1798 to 1816, he evidently maintained an interest in botany, and was in contact with a number of people in Canton who were actively engaged in plant collecting. On his return to England George Thomas Staunton settled at Leigh Park, Havant, and from 1820 onwards planned a landscape garden in the great eighteenth century tradition. Among the follies in his park he included a Turkish Tent, a Corinthian bridge, a Chinese bridge and a Chinese boat house.

Documentary evidence shows Staunton's contact with contemporary botanists and his prominence in the horticultural circles of the day. The garden is now part of the Sir George Staunton Country Park run by Portsmouth City Council[9].

The eighteenth century taste for landscape gardening developed into the nineteenth century fashion for horticulture. The content of the garden dominated its overall design and the gardenesque succeeded picturesque. William Cobbett of Botley (see page 80) in *The English Gardener*, 1828, wrote:

> '. . . the fashion has for years been in favour of borders wherein flowers of the greatest brilliancy are planted so disposed as to form a regular series higher and higher as they approach the back part, or the middle of the border; and so selected as to ensure a succession of blossom from the earliest months of the spring until the coming frost'.

New plants were being brought to this country from the Andes, the Himalayas and later China and Japan. The 19th century saw a huge increase in selective breeding and the creation of hybrids. Hampshire was a particular centre for extensive work on rhododendrons especially in the 1820's by Gowen at Highclere. The interest in new plants was also transmitted through a number of colour plate magazines and the opening of public botanic gardens. It has been pointed out that 'the magazines spread the message of the new ideology of gardening, but it was Head Gardeners who interpreted it.[10] The Head Gardener replaced the Landscape Gardener in importance.

In the 1840's picturesque theories were again discussed particularly with regard to the introduction of colour into gardens. Highclere was planted with shrubs for autumn colour and also with rhododendrons and other American shrubs whose reflections in the lake reminded some spectators 'of some of Claude Loraine's glowing sunsets'. In his recent book, *Victorian Gardens*, Brent Elliott has demonstrated the importance of William Wildsmith of Heckfield Place in late Victorian garden history:

> "By 1880 he had emerged as the most celebrated gardener of his generation, the author of regular columns in both the Gardeners' Chronicle and the Garden; Heckfield was repeatedly discussed in the

9. Acknowledgements to Derek Gladwyn and Michael Crane, Bristol City Museums.

10. Elliott, Brent, *Victorian Gardens*, Batsford, 1986, p. 13.

magazines, and opened to the public for a week every year, thus making his experiments accessible to a wide audience."[11]

Wildsmith recommended four styles of summer flowering gardening: colour massing, the carpet, the neutral, through use of succulents and the sub-tropical. His 'beau ideal' was a mixture of the four. He recommended softer less dominant colours and a denser and more profuse planting of beds. In 1882 the stone baskets and beds on the terrace at Heckfield were:

". . .filled chiefly with the intensely bright double Casctus Dahlia Juaresii, and the rich single variety Paragon, not formally staked, but each plant affording support to the other, the whole forming a great tangled mass of flowers. These were relieved by groups of white and golden Marguerites, Heliotropes, &c., with Tropaeolums scrambling among them and falling over the sides here and there, as if escaping from an overladen receptacle. The plants appear to have been inserted, and then as regards their floral outline left to take their chance. Their growth has been a floral struggle as if to present the survival of the fittest; and the freedom, almost wildness, of the arrangement was not only pleasing in itself, but by force of contrast the trim and highly finished compact beds were shown to great advantage".[12]

For twenty years Heckfield was famous as a training centre for many gardeners who became well known in the next generation and the influence of his teaching at Heckfield spread to other gardens in Hampshire. At Dogsmersfield his pupil George Trinder produced beds "filled in with every conceivable mathematical design worked out in the flowers or foliage plants and at Elvetham T. Jones planted immense beds of formal design but planted in 'such a loose, natural manner as to completely destroy all formality"[13].

In contrast, Minley Manor was a geometric designed by Robert T. Veitch and his landscaper, F.W. Meyer. The house was in the style of a French chateau and a complex parterre was laid out in miniature conifers representing the family crest. Dwarfed hollies in different colours were illuminated by electric light at night.[14]

By the end of the nineteenth century there was a revival of the idea that an architect should involve himself in the planning of the garden surrounding a house of his own design. Unlike the Brownian scheme of house and park late Victorian and Edwardian taste set the house firmly in elaborate gardens of flowerbeds, lawns and terraces and a complementary style was important.

In 1898 Sir Lionel Philips purchased the estate at Tylney. He was a South African diamond and gold millionaire and immediately commissioned Seldon Wornum to make alterations to the house. These works went on between 1899 and 1902 by which time the house had been almost entirely rebuilt.

Seldon Wornum laid out the Italian Terrace Garden, and possibly the Dutch Garden, but between 1901-5 R. Weir Schultz was called in "to lay out the beds and formal parts of a luxurious garden layout including orangery, greenhouses, summer house, boathouse etc.". R. Weir Schultz was an architect linked with the Arts and Crafts movement, and had built up a reputation for garden design.

Sir Lionel Phillips spent a great deal of money and care on the garden and a huge number and variety of trees and shrubs were planted. An article in the *Gardeners' Chronicle* (1905) describes the luxurance and extent of

11. *Op. cit.*, p. 203.
12. *Op. cit.*, pp. 204-205.
13. *Ibid.*
14. *Op. cit.* p. 216.

Tylney Hall, Rotherwick,
National Monuments Record

the garden as well as his additions in the park. It describes the avenue in the direction of Hook Station 'recently planted with Chestnuts', the avenue leading to Rotherwick 'with limes planted about 25 years ago', the grass glade to the west of the house, 'well furnished with Seguoia gigantea, and Pseudotsuga douglasii 40 feet high', and on the east side on the site of a former carriage drive 'Douglas fir, Cedrus Atlantica, Abies concolur, and Abies nordmanniana have been planted'.[15]

An area to the north of the house around two ponds was made into a woodland garden with a winding path through clumps of rhododendrons and other flowering shrubs, naturalised bulbs and bamboos.

The terrace of the Italian garden was planted out with bright bedding plants, and there were lots of roses:

'. . . a hedge on each side of a broad carriage drive 200 yards long is composed entirely of climbing varieties. . . Pink Roamer covers the low south wall of the plant stores. . . near the house is a large square planted with tea and hybrid tea varieties, and in the grounds a circulat plot 40 yards wide encircled with a yew hedge contains hybrid perpetuals with crimson rambler trailing over the central arches. . . The yellow Banksian rose is luxuriating on the walls of the house. . .'[16]

In 1906 Gertrude Jekyll was asked to provide R. Weir Schultz with design and planting plans for a Wild Garden to the south of the Kitchen Garden. She never visited the site but drew up several plans for the garden based on surveys provided by Schultz who had already designed the two ponds and some planting. Her plans survive and include flower borders along the south wall and in front of the Orangery. Very little remains of her splendid garden as it was redesigned during the 1940's by Woods of Taplow. Fortunately Jekyll's planting plans, some written descriptions and old photographs give a rich impression of its scale and luxuriance.

Sir Reginald Blomfield, architect and author of *The Formal Garden*, used Hampton Court as a model for his 1908-9 mansion at Moundsmere built for Wilfred Buckley. Blomfield laid out the garden in a correspondingly formal style with high clipped yew hedges, adding herbaceous borders.

A local architect, H. Inigo Triggs, wrote *Formal Gardens in England and*

15. *The Gardeners' Chronicle*, I, 1905, p. 257.
16. *Ibid.*

Scotland, 1901-2, and a series of books on garden craft between 1902 and 1913. In 1910, he built his own house, Little Boarhunt at Liphook with a sunken garden in a neo-Elizabethan style with central pool and canal. He designed several other gardens in the area and some of his work is illustrated in Gertrude Jekyll and Weaver's *Gardens for Small Country Houses*.

G.A. Kitchin, another local architect, who specialised in the restoration of local buildings such as the Chapel at Twyford School and the Chesil Rectory, Winchester, bought a small cottage in Compton, Winchester, in 1894. Within fifteen years he had transformed the gardens of Compton End with a succession of walks enclosed by high yew hedges and herbaceous borders. His architectural and gardening style echoes Blomfield and Jekyll in its balance between the vernacular and a return to the formal, Jacobean taste.

Thomas Hayton Mawson published his *Art and Craft of Garden Making* in 1900 and, although already an established garden designer, attracted the attention of new and influential clients. He acknowledged the influence of Repton on his career and coined the term 'landscape architect' to describe himself maintaining that an English vernacular style must maintain awareness of the landscape.

In 1907, Mawson worked at New Place, Botley, for which Edward Lutyens designed the house. The owner insisted that Mawson, rather than Lutyens, design the garden but in his autobiography, he wrote:

> 'Looking back I am certain that Lutyens without me would have achieved a great success; and, on the other hand I am sure I could have done a finer garden had I been entirely untrammelled'.

Mawson worked at Walhampton for Lord St. Cyr where Norman Shaw had added a Victorian wing to the house and may have designed the sunken garden and raised terrace (shown on the 1907 revision of the 1867 Ordnance Survey map). Mawson opened up the landscape to the south east of the house, probably adding the large fountain with a bronze figure of Mercury and much of the other garden statuary. A fine loggia was added linking the house to the grotto (see page 13) and the forecourt with its pierced open work walling was constructed. The forecourt was further elaborated by two sets of gate piers with elaborate wrought iron gates. His plans for the garden are in Kendal Record Office and include further designs for a pergola, rose temple and lynch gate.[17]

Mawson was also involved with what might have been one of the most dramatic and romantic projects in the area had it ever been realised. The department store millionaire, Gordon Selfridge, with his architect Philip Tilden, envisaged a castle to crown Hengistbury Head (now in Dorset) with ramparts and terraces linked to gardens, parkland, sheltered lowlands, extensive orchards, vegetable gardens and a nursery. Mawson notes in his autobiography that he was too practical a designer for Selfridge's fantastic schemes. Mawson died in 1933 but his firm continued to work in the area until the Second World War. Edwin Lutyens is the most dominant rival to Mawson as an Art and Crafts architect who designed gardens to accompany their houses. His work with the garden designer and author Gertrude Jekyll is a famous and remarkable partnership.

Lutyens designed the unique house called Marshcourt near Stockbridge. Not only is it closely related to its site, on a spur overlooking the Test Valley, but it also reflects the geology being mainly constructed of chalk. The garden is an elaborate scheme of surrounding terraces,

17. Acknowledgement to Harriet Jordan, David Mawson, Colin Stanfield and Kay Welham.

balustrades, walls and pergolas. Jekyll was certainly commissioned to work on the gardens and, although her plans for the Wild Garden, approach road, entrance to the kitchen and farm gardens survive, those for the formal, terrace gardens do not.

The Manor House, Upton Grey was designed by Ernest Newton for Charles Holmes, editor of *The Studio*, an Arts and Crafts magazine. Gertrude Jekyll designed a Wild Garden, nuttery and a formal garden with a pergola and dry stone wall terraces. Her planting plan survives and the present owners are restoring the whole scheme.

On the outskirts of Southampton at Grove Place, Nursling, Captain B. de la Sales la Terriere set out new gardens during the 1920's on the site of an earlier walled garden. He furnished the garden with a great amount of garden statuary including two figures of Woden and Thor by the 17th century English sculptor Rysbrack which he had bought in the sale at Stowe in 1921.

L. Rome Guthrie, *Design for Townhill Gardens*, British Architectural Association, Drawings Collection

Also on the outskirts of Southampton is Townhill Park, originally a small house in a modest park acquired by the first Lord Swaythling in 1897. The second Lord Swaythling commissioned L. Rome Guthrie to transform it into a country house in the Italianate style. Plans for the house and garden were interrupted by the First World War but continued afterwards.

Guthrie certainly designed the formal Italianate garden surrounded by a pergola walk leading around to a summerhouse with a red pantiled roof set axially. His plans suggest that Guthrie seems to have designed a number of alternative arrangements for the gardens and Gertrude Jekyll designed the planting. Without any evidence it is difficult to decide who was responsible for the final design but it was no doubt due to the discussion and inter-action between Guthrie the architect, Gertrude Jekyll the plantswoman and artist and Lord Swaythling, himself an enthusiastic gardener and plantsman. Jekyll's planting plans for the sunken garden and for the two square herb gardens survive.

Of great importance are the arboretum planted out at Townhill Park from 1912 onwards and the nearby Marlhill Copse, (previously called Swan Copse). Marlhill Copse an area of some five hectares, was laid out as a woodland garden. The oak woodland was thinned and glades were cut through making a light oak canopy with ideal conditions for growing many of the recently introduced ornamental trees and shrubs, notably rhododendrons, magnolias, Northofagus and camellias. When the third Lord Swaythling inherited the estate in 1927 he and his head gardener, Mr. F. Rose, became interest in hybridising rhododendrons. Between 1932 and 1946 over thirteen varieties received Awards of Merit from the Royal Horticultural Society and by 1933 an article was published about Marlhill Copse in *Country Life*. Particular mention was made of Lilium giganteum growing in the woodland.

A list of the rhododendron crosses from Townhill Park are:

'Mary Swaythling'	1934
Imperator	1934
Rhododendron pumilum	1935
Rhododendron megeratum	1936
Rhododendron deliense	1935
'David'	1939
'Agnes'	1943
'Julie'	1944
'Marcia'	1944
'Dot'	1945
Rhododendron 'Albatross'	Townhill form 1945
Rhododendron 'Redcap' Variety 'Townhill Park'	1945
'Margaret Dunn'	1946

At Embley Park, near Romsey there were similar developments. During the 1930's Mr. J.J. Crosfield set out in oak woodland a garden specialising in rhododendrons but with other exotics. The house dates from 1825 and was built by Florence Nightingale's father and the parkland dates from the 1780's when Sir William Heathcote, son-in-law of the previous owner, laid out the park in the landscape style with follies, including a grotto, rustic cottages and an American garden. The existing woodland garden, which is being restored, dates from Mr. Crosfield's period of residence. Not only was there a wealth of rhododendrons but there was also a heath garden and a mass of exotic trees and shrubs which included pieris, enkianthus, kalmias and magnolias. Some rhododendron crosses were also developed at Embley:

Blue Diamond	1935
Cool Haven (raised at Embley but named by Hilliers)	1945
Coronation Day	1937
Fire Glow	1935
Jersey Cream	1937
Tally Ho	1933
Touchstone	1937

A deciduous hybrid azalea Embley Crimson was developed and the Sourbus aucuparia 'Embley' was first recognised by Hillier at Embley Park.

The firm of Hilliers was founded in 1854 by Edwin Hillier who had worked as a gardener at great houses such as Syon and Studley Royal. He bought the West Hill Nursery in Winchester in 1870 and his son Edwin Lawrence built up the collection of trees and shrubs that has made the firm famous. Harold Hillier, grandson of the founder, became an authority on trees and shrubs in the temperate zone and the Hillier Arboretum at Jermyns, Ampfield includes about 14,000 species. The arboretum was given to Hampshire County Council in 1977.

Rhododendrons and azaleas are associated internationally with Exbury and the de Rothschild family in the New Forest. In the 1920's rhododendrons were being planted in large quantities in muncipal parks and private gardens throughout Britain to give colour and variety. At the early part of the decade Lionel de Rothschild, introduced to this part of Hampshire through his friendship with John Montagu of Beaulieu, purchased the Exbury estate and began to plant its 200 acres and develop it as the most complete collection of rhododendrons species in the country. The Exbury strain of azaleas are internationally famous and over 1200 new hybrids have been created.

Continuing the tradition of important garden literature written in Hampshire, Sir Ralph Dutton of Hinton Ampner wrote *The English Garden* in 1937. He also wrote *A Hampshire Manor* in 1968 which tells the history of his house and the creation of its garden. From his father's death in 1935, Ralph Dutton developed Hinton Ampner into one of the finest of all modern formal gardens. He records the vestial remains of a Tudor garden, a kitchen garden created before 1793 and a terrace bowling green or 'troco' mentioned in a survey of 1649. An early 18th century avenue was 'clumped' about 1793. At the beginning of this century, when Ralph Dutton was a boy, he described the garden as "quite an attractive example of mid-Victorian design". His grandparents filled many small flowerbeds with "inevitable scarlet geraniums and lobelia". His mother swept away the weeping ashes, maples and standard roses and replaced them with Dorothy Perkins, Crimson Rambler and hybrid teas.

Sir Ralph writes that he took to heart Pope's famous lines from his *Epistle to Lord Burlington*:

> "Let not each beauty ev'ry where be spy'd
> Where half the skill is decently to hide;
> He gains all points, who pleasingly confounds,
> Surprises, varies, and conceals the Bounds"

and translated them from their application in a great park to a garden. Hinton Ampner remains a superbly architectural garden of long grassy walks, yew hedges, fine trees and vistas leading to classical statuary.

Today, the importance of good design applied to landscape or garden is no longer restricted to private estates. Major new buildings such as those designed by Arup Associates for IBM in Portsmouth and Wiggins Teape in Basingstoke have incorporated magnificent planting schemes by James Russell. On a more modest scale, but a great achievement, is the work of Awbridge Infants School. Here children have been taught about the importance of herb gardens in the Tudor period and then, using a computer, have planned the pattern of a knot garden, recreated the design in their school grounds and planted it with herbs. These grew successfully, were harvested and the profits used to buy more plants. This project illustrates perfectly the intentions behind the 'Learning through Landscape' scheme.

Increasingly, the public is visiting gardens such as Broadlands and Stratfield Saye, the National Trust's the Vyne, West Green, Mottisfont and Hinton Ampner or plantsmen's gardens such as Jenkyn Place and Spinners. The large, landscaped parks contrasting with the superb modern plantsmen's gardens and a new emphasis on planting schemes in public and commercial projects suggest that 'Learning through Landscapes' is applicable to all of us.

Above:
Watering cans, etc., Private Collection

Left:
Earthenware thumb-pot, Private Collection

The Re-creation of a Medieval & a Sixteenth Century Garden in Hampshire

DR. SYLVIA LANDSBERG

"Imagination bodies forth the forms of things unknown, turns them to shapes, and gives to airy nothing a local habitation and a name".

(Midsummer Night's Dream).

Who better than Shakespeare to define the art of period garden re-creation? The following account describes the process by which two such re-creations were achieved, the thirteenth century Queen Eleanor's garden in Winchester, and the sixteenth century Tudor Garden in Southampton.

The longer a dwelling place has been continuously inhabited the more it will have changed from time to time in accordance with current fashion. However, the earlier the period of a garden, the less likely it is that design details such as plant lists, will have been recorded, and much less likely that any will have survived. There is therefore no location in Hampshire where there are sufficient records to restore a garden earlier than the seventeenth century.

To build up a mental idea of early gardens we have to piece together mere fragments of information. This results in an overall picture which can be reproduced in book form, to satisfy our intellectual appetite. But we can also *re-create* actual gardens in the same way even if there is not enough knowledge to *restore* an actual garden which once existed. In this way we can again experience the sensual pleasures of *being in* such gardens in addition to reading about them. Thus we can view again the knot gardens described in Parkinson's 'Paridisi in Sole', smell again a living carpet of camomile, pennyroyal and thyme so loved by Bacon. The medieval poet's 'It smote me swoot right to the heart's root' is expressive but cannot provide the total experience of the overwhelming perfume of a bouquet collected from a medieval garden and kept overnight in a small room.

How does the designer go about re-creating such gardens about which little or no evidence survives? First there is a period of searching the literature, which should not be rushed since one goes on learning something new daily. Had we known more about the sites chosen for Queen Eleanor's Garden or the Tudor House Garden the job would have been simpler. 'Let three herbaria be made', and 'a little garden', respectively, were the only contemporary remarks describing early garden features on these sites that we had to go on. Time is also necessary before the mental chaos, caused by the horticultural and historical rag-bag that one accumulates, can be turned into a clear design — a process psychologically known as 're-grouping of skills'. Seventeenth century Parkinson experienced this process, which is part of all creation. 'Where I have meandered, others will later walk in a straight line' he says, finally giving up the classification of seventeenth century roses in despair.

One gradually develops a list of works to be read, and from it one makes a shorter list with more focus. Each of these works will yield further avenues of research. Soon one is reading about habits and fashions, political and philosophical background, arts and crafts etc. of the period, quite apart from the present, mushrooming, state of garden history knowledge.

In addition to present day writers, and contemporary writers such as Gerard, Hill, Lawson, Worlidge and Parkinson there are many primary sources, including manuscripts and plans, to be read and interpreted. If one is lucky an historian such as John Harvey will have been before, transcribing the manuscripts. His Winchester College transcriptions and translations reveal pleasant details such as the fact that the name of one of the medieval gardeners was Thomas Daisy. To read the actual damp-stained faded ink letter of one sixteenth century writer incarcerated in 'the Clink' in London, causes one to re-tread the past with reverence. Here he is instructing his steward to plant the arbours before his Northampton house is constructed, so that the trees will be mature when the house is finished. Or again, giving instructions to plant periwinkle and wild strawberry beneath the roses damask and red, to save the weeding.

Archaeological accounts can reveal the skeletons of past gardens, and aerial photography shows up ghosts unseen on the ground. For instance, is the fascinating crescent-shape at Elvetham, near Yately, the site of the golden garden pageant laid on for Queen Elizabeth on a crescent-shaped lake, of which a full eyewitness account exists? The detective designer notes, by the way, that the spiral path of the mount was planted with privet.

Fountain and Pool at Queen Eleanor's Garden, Joyce Moore

The designer of a re-created garden will have to communicate with a vast array of 'experts'. Letters, phone calls, visits to libraries, nurseries, craftsmen and workshops, actual sites, conversations with garden history friends, everyone brimming with enthusiasm for their work and yours, often no two minds agreeing, or knowing the answer.

While all this knowledge has been accumulating the mind has also been addressing the practicalities of the project. What are the restrictions of the proposed site itself, who is paying and how much for construction and maintenance? How much time for investigation? What is the purpose of the garden? Will the project benefit from an archaeological investigation first, as was the case at The Great Hall, Winchester, where excavations revealed not a garden, but an unknown room of King Stephen's Palace.

Gradually the plant list firms up from perusing such books as Gerard's 'Herball', and working drawings can be produced from the exquisitely painted manuscripts of 500 - 600 years ago, the more crude medium of woodcuts of 400 years ago, or elegant etchings of 300 years ago. Sometimes a magnifying glass is necessary. For instance the cane carnation supports at Tudor House are copied from the tiny 1/4 inch illustration in Thomas Hill's 'Gardener's Labyrinth'. Similarly a lens is necessary to fully appreciate the useful detail of David Loggan's seventeenth century etchings.

A firm commitment to actual layout must finally be made. Those new ideas which a bad night's sleep often has the habit of producing at breakfast time, often recorded on backs of envelopes, have to be sifted through. The designer's own subjective decisions may have to be taken where there is doubt. A simple rule is to give authenticity first priority, then aesthetics, then practicability. Even so an overall feeling of the period in terms of gardens is difficult to interpret. Whereas a book chapter can end and a new page can start when knowledge becomes hazy, the garden plan has to account for every relentlessly demanding square inch. What level will it be, of what constructed? What will be built on it, or what will clothe it? The design for the bronze falcon for the fountain in Queen Eleanor's Garden required equal precision. No single thirteenth century bronze falcon exists in the country, so the drawings from which it was carved were based on thirteenth century book illustrations, misericord wood carvings of other birds, stylisation of sculptures from a gold thirteenth century dove in the British Museum, and lectern birds. Various details and positions from falcons photographed in flight at the Andover Hawk Conservancy were used in the recreation. Twelfth century falcon bells can be seen in the British Museum, and feather detail and the 'feel' of the bird came from the early fourteenth century carved wooden falcon in Winchester Cathedral, bearing in mind that its head may not be the original.

At this stage the designer can now produce an artist's impression of the garden from which a model can be made if required, giving an exciting thrill of *déjà-vu*. This can help to show up flaws. For instance in the exhibited model of Queen Eleanor's Garden the raised curb edge of the channel, although flush with the turf, could have caused people to trip where it crossed the paved area next to the pool, so it had to be altered.

Queen Eleanor's Garden, Winchester, Joyce Moore

Discussions with quantity surveyors and contractors are the next step and a timescale is laid down so that one item will not hold up another. Tenders for construction go out. The designer has got the garden out of books onto the drawing board, but a co-ordinator is essential to get it off the board on to the ground, or to ensure that attention is paid to details. For instance, at Winchester one could not let the bulldozer knock down the thirteenth century Hall pillars. Again at Winchester a path had to be altered to avoid cutting into an unknown spaghetti junction of pipes and wires beneath the ground, and instructions had to be given that carpentry work on the Law Courts wall *must* be stopped by 10 a.m. at certain risk of an injunction from an irate judge within, etc. Another year or two of such daily problems and the garden will be ready for its official opening.

The process just described has been gone through for Queen Eleanor's Garden and the Tudor Garden. An illustrated leaflet, with historical context, layout, description of features, and plant list, is available for each garden, and this information need not be repeated here. However a few overall remarks follow.

Queen Eleanor's Garden, The Great Hall, Winchester

A thirteenth century re-creation of a castle pleasure garden, the only authentic one in Britain. Opened by Her Majesty the Queen Mother on July 8, 1986, in brilliant sun to the fanfare of trumpets, with every rose and lily flowering. It was the inspiration of the Hampshire Gardens Trust to turn this tiny wedge some 90 × 30 ft. into a garden of the period of building of the Great Hall. The latter was built by Henry III, and the garden is named after his Queen, Eleanor of Provence and also after Queen Eleanor of Castile, wife of his son Edward I. All of them would have once trodden this ground. The garden was funded through Hampshire County Council, who owned the land and it was constructed through the County Architect's Department, with Senior County Architect Brian Grayling as architect, co-ordinator and trouble shooter. Sylvia Landsberg was the designer, with John Harvey as consultant and co-designer.

The budget, though generous, did not greatly exceed the cost of merely York paving the area, and was augmented by grants from the Southern Tourist Board, and the Stanley Smith Horticultural Trust. Apart from gardening skills, it incorporates carpentry, woodcarving, trelliswork, stonemasonry, plumbing and leadwork, bronze-casting, gilding, oak-shingle roofing, and dove-keeping. In the absence of any knowledge of the actual garden on the site, the present garden has been built up from fragmentary quotations of the 7 or 8 royal palace and castle gardens of Henry III and Edward I. Now once again it is possible, to sit, as they did, in the sun against the warm Great Hall wall, hear the fountain splashing, savour the perfumes of roses red and white, Madonna lilies, etc, and many herbs with the white doves flying overhead.

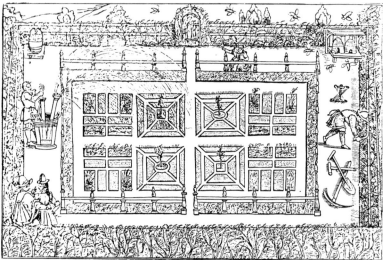

A small enclosed garden: Thomas Hill 'The Gardener's Labyrinth' 1577. Balustrades and Herb Bed arrangements for Tudor House have been adapted from this illustration

The Tudor Garden, Tudor House, Bugle Street, Southampton

The inspiration of the Friends of Southampton Museums and Art Galleries, researched and designed by Sylvia Landsberg, the Tudor House Garden is a collection of features of ornamental gardens of the Tudor reign

(1485 - 1603). The plants are a selection of those grown in the period, each displayed in the way it would have been used. It was completed in 1982, and measures approximately 40 × 30 ft. The garden was funded by many private donations, from 50 pence to £100, with gifts from several institutions and generous grants from the Stanley Smith Horticultural Trust, the Ernest Cook Educational Trust, the Hampshire County Council, and the Southern Tourist Board.

It is owned and maintained by Southampton City Council. The garden was built on a shoe-string budget and was constructed by two City gardeners, who wheeled all the materials through the polished halls of Tudor House. Many crafts, as in Queen Eleanor's Garden, are exhibited. The herb design is taken from the English version of Estienne and Liebault's 'Country Farm'. In comparison to the peace and overall uplifting feeling of the Winchester garden, the Tudor Garden in full season is brilliant, fussy, contrived, perfumed.

Other Seventeenth Century Gardens

The Petersfield Physic Garden, High Street, Petersfield is shortly to be constructed. The aim of the garden is to encourage plant conservation by developing an interest in our floral history. The plot is a donation from Major John Bowen who has specified its purpose. It will be administered by a trust set up for the purpose, and which will raise funds for it.

Finally, although just outside the Hampshire boundaries, the beautiful gardens of seventeenth century Cranborne Manor should not be missed. Replanted *con amore* by the Countess of Salisbury, from plans and plant lists of John Tradescant who, subsequent to Gerard, was employed by the forebears of the present Earl and Countess. The gardens include a mount, knot and herb garden.

FORMAL GARDENS
in Hampshire

KRYSTYNA BILIKOWSKI

Although the great landscapes of the Restoration period were largely swept away by landscaped parks in the "English style" developed principally by "Capability" Brown and his followers in the eighteenth century, documentary material and illustrations, in association with fieldwork, chart the development and persistence of gardens in a formal style from the post civil war period to the early twentieth century. Parklands around country houses were created until the early twentieth century, and although the landscape style persisted, the middle years of the nineteenth century saw a return to a formal style of gardening, which differed from the earlier seventeenth and eighteenth century formal landscapes both in character and scale.

The main impetus in both the design and planting of gardens occurred after the Restoration; being drawn mainly from abroad. Trading increased, and with it there was an increase in the introduction of exotic plants. In turn this resulted in a considerable change in the skills and development of the nursery business. Architecture flourished and with it, for the first time, a design consciousness which was expressed in the countryside through the ordering of estates with formal rides, copses, etc.

Topiary, Melchet Court,
National Monuments Record

Southwick Park, near Portsmouth is a good example of such a site. After the dissolution of Southwick Priory in 1539, it was acquired by John White. The gardens were illustrated by Kip in 1714[1] and may have been drawn still earlier. Entitled "the Seat of Richard Norton", they picture the gardens as set out by the Norton family in the late 1600's. They show that a fashionable garden in the formal, continental style had been laid out next to the house. The mansion was set out partly on the foundations of the priory with an entrance forecourt, formal carriage circle, garden terraces with a central basin, flanking parterres and an orangery. All that survives today beyond the ruins of the secularised priory are the earthworks of the garden terraces which can be seen magnificently from the air in the southern part of Southwick Park.

1. Knyff, Leonard and Kip, Johannes, *Britannia Illustrata or views of several of the Queen's Places and also of the principal seats of the nobility and gentry of Great Britain*, London, 1714-15.

Marsh Court, Lucinda Lambton

Tudor House Garden, Southampton,
Heather Angel

17th. tapestry, *Hunting, Games and
Amusements,* (detail) Breamore House

Jenkyn Place, Heather Angel

Another site of which only earthworks remain is at Chilton Candover. No illustration or maps survive but enough can be discerned from field work to give some idea of the layout. The mansion house "Worsley Hall" was set out during the 1690's and by the mid eighteenth century was almost entirely forgotten. It has been described as one of the forgotten palaces of Hampshire.[2] In 1662 the estate of Chilton Candover was bought by the Worsley family and in the 1690's Sir Robert Worsley was engaged in land purchases and engrossing. He completed a 'Grand Tour' of Europe in 1690 and married Frances Thynne. She was the daughter of the 1st Viscount of Weymouth who created vast formal gardens at Longleat. After their marriage the Worsleys lived at Chilton Candover where Sir Robert set out the formal gardens. A sunken lane which runs over the crest of the downs leads from a woodland and up the other side of the Candover valley to Juniper Hill, and its southern part is lined by a yew avenue. To the north of the house the avenue divided into a "patte d'oie"; again lined by yew trees, some of which still remain. In all, this formal avenue was some half a mile long.

Robert Worsley is best known for his work at Appeldurcombe House, Isle of Wight, where he extensively rebuilt and laid out new gardens from 1701 onwards. There is no evidence left of the vast formal landscape which he created at Appeldurcombe and which was swept away by "Capability" Brown in the 1770's, but what may be significant is his choice of architect. Worsley appointed John James to design the new house at Appeldurcombe.

John James who translated d'Argenville's seminal work *The Theory and Practice of Gardening* into English in 1712 was one of the leading architects of the day but as with many such figures we know very little about him and it is difficult to ascribe works to him. He was an Assistant Surveyor under Christopher Wren and from 1736-1745 was surveyor to the fabric of Westminster Abbey. He built a house for himself in Hampshire at Warbrook, near Eversley and laid out there a small French style garden with canals and radiating woodland paths, which adhered to the principles discussed in the "Theory and Practice". Amongst those subscribing to his book, and thereby funding its publication, were John Aislabie who laid out the extensive formal gardens at Studley Royal, James Brydges of Canons, and the Earl of Carlisle of Castle Howard. Also among the subscribers were two Worsleys; Sir Robert Worsley who employed James at Appeldurcombe and who set out the gardens at Chilton Candover, and his cousin Sir James Worsley of "Pilewell" (Pylewell, near Lymington). The gardens at Pylewell were illustrated by Badeslade and Rocque in 1739.[3] Although some allowance must be made for artistic licence, and all such topographical views must be treated with a degree of caution, some of the features of the design at Pylewell remain. There is a broad central vista to the Isle of Wight across the parkland through flanking belts of trees. There is a semi-circular, formal enclosure which may be traced in the outline of the surviving formal balustrade.

Apart from Warbrook, James was definitely commissioned to work at Herriard House, although here his designs were confined to proposals for the house, George London designing the gardens.

George London, who died in 1714, was one of the famous partnership of London and Wise, nurserymen of Brompton Road. He is generally accredited with the setting out of many of the gardens shown in contemporary illustrations of the time. The London and Wise business

2. *Hampshire Notes and Queries*
3. Badeslade, Thomas and Rocque, J. *Vitruvius Brittanicus* vol. 4. London, 1739. Reprinted 1967.

spawned many gardeners who, in their own right, moved on to design famous gardens. One such was Stephen Switzer, who worked with Wise at Blenheim.

Stephen Switzer (1682-1745) was born in East Stratton, eight miles from Winchester and trained as a gardener at Stratton House. Stratton House was one of the country seats of William Russell, the 5th Earl and 1st Duke of Bedford. Sir William Russell had already paid a great deal of attention to his gardens at Woburn before the Restoration. In addition, his London residence at Bedford House was well known for its extensive formal gardens. Stephen Switzer is one of the main sources for our knowledge of George London in his book *The Nobleman, Gentleman and Gardeners Recreation* printed in 1715 and later republished as *Ichnographia Rustica*.[4] He also pays homage to Sir William Russell:

"one of the best of Masters as well as Gardeners . . . his works in Gardening were none of the smallest . . . he made Stratton about 7 miles from Winchester his seat; and his gardens there some of the best that were made at that Time, such indeed as have mock'd some that have been since done".

The park and gardens at Stratton were certainly laid out by Lord William and Lady Rachel Russell between 1669-1683 and were further kept by Lady Rachel after her husband's execution in 1683 until her own death in 1723. A survey of 1730, complete with map, made for their son describes their

4.   Switzer, Stephen *Ichnographia Rustica or The Nobleman, Gentleman and Gardener's Recreation.*

work in extending the house with two wings, building laundries, brewhouses and service buildings. They made orchards, gardens and avenues, planted groves, wildernesses "and other ornaments to adorn and accommodate this beautiful and pleasant seat". The survey adds "he also pulled down part of the town or hamlet of Stratton and laid it into his deer park". This initial phase of depopulation preceded a later one in the 19th century when Sir Francis Baring owned the estate. The village of East Stratton once extended virtually up to the mansion house itself, or in part into the area called "The Furlong" which, separated by a road enclosed in 1664, was surrounded by a park pale and made into part of the park.

The landscape set out around the house was very formal. The Roman Road was lined by an avenue of trees and called "Love Walk", only recently partly destroyed by construction works for the M3 motorway. Formal plantings were set out in "The Plantation" and "The Firs". The latter consisted of specimen trees. Lady Rachel refers to them in a letter of 1703 in her account of the Great Storm thought to have been one of the worst to affect England:

"The Fir Grove is entirely broken and torn up by the roots.. . . ."[5]

In *Ichnographia Rustica* Switzer discusses at length the cultivation of types of fir, this gives some indication of a craze which was popular during this period; the growing of fir trees. Evergreens were popular during this period and it must be realised that traditionally there were a limited number of evergreens either among the native flora of this country or commonly grown as exotics until the late 1600's. The tree grown at Stratton was probably the silver fir Abies alba which was, until the introduction of the Douglas Fir in 1955, the tallest growing tree in this country. Contemporary with the fir grove at Stratton was the setting out of the great fir tree avenue at Herriard, shown on a 1730 estate map, and possibly a part of London's design.

At Highclere Park the formal layout of the grounds before the "improvements" made by Brown are known from a map of 1795 which is entitled "The grounds as they were in 1768". This plan, together with a manuscript in the British Library and the surviving follies and field evidence, leads to a full picture of the formal layout. The gardens were laid out in the early 1700's by Robert Herbert, who inherited the estate. The formal landscape which he set out around the house was dotted with ornamental follies. Unfortunately the paucity of documentary evidence for this period in the extensive Highclere archives means that the designer of the layout is unknown. In addition to the follies there were serpentine walks, lawns, a ha-ha, avenues, drives and groves. Highclere is important in that, whereas at other sites some of the remains of formal gardens can only be found by tracing boundary lines, tree groups or earthworks, at Highclere most of the garden follies still exist. Heaven's Gate was a monumental arch standing in a "little scrubby wood of whitethorns and oaks" on the top of Siddown Hill. A large avenue bordered the Long Walk, some half a mile in length, and led up to Heaven's Gate from Highclere house. At present this feature of the early formal landscape is overgrown, although originally the slopes of Siddown Hill were downland and the folly was clearly visible from the mansion. The garden temple, Jackdaws Castle, forms an eyecatcher from the house across the lawns. There was also a wooden Tuscan temple.

Also dating from the first half of the 18th century was the landscape set

5. *Letters of Rachel, Lady Russell*, Longman, 1853.

The Water Garden, Brockenhurst,
National Monuments Record

out around Tylney Hall, near Rotherwick. Tylney Hall was a large mansion house built about 1700 by Frederick Tylney, and already by this date it was set in a park. A most beautiful and detailed estate map of 1774 shows the extensive landscape set out around the new house, as distinct from the "Old House" which was presumably the surviving mansion house dating from the mid sixteenth century. The second Earl of Tylney spend most of his life abroad, although he was responsible for commissioning the excellent estate map and it is probable that the landscape design was laid out by his father, Richard Child, Viscount Castlemain, the first Earl. Probably, the design was never completed the family's main country seat being at Wanstead House, Redbridge, London. A central vista was aligned along an avenue which led to Rotherwick Common, with a series of long, formal Versailles type canals stretching beyond. Old field boundaries can be seen in the parkland, and further formal avenues and groves, or perhaps orchards were laid out around the house. A design by Sir William Chambers (1726-96) for an Octagon temple for "The Earl of Tilney" in the Soane Museum, may be for their seat at Wanstead.

The revival of the formal garden as a style during the nineteenth century was due to the attention paid by the architect to the design of the gardens which surrounded the house. The rise of the landscape profession was due in part to Brown and his followers who were responsible for the "English landscape style" applied to gardens as far away as Russia and America.

Repton, by popularising the concept of specialist gardens, foreshadowed the great revival of formality in the nineteenth century. However most garden designers were either from the architectural profession or were horticulturalists. Cranbury Park, Hursley has a garden set out mainly by the architect J.B. Papworth (1775-1847). Unfortunately the estate papers for Cranbury do not survive, but the work was probably done for Thomas Chamberlayne who remodelled much of the estate. A grotto in the gardens commemmorates a visit to Cranbury by Wordsworth (1770-1850) and on a tablet set above a spring source in the grotto is a poem, said to have been composed by him:

> "Gentle reader view in me
> An emblem of true charity
> Who while my bounty I bestow
> Am neither heard nor seen to flow
> For every drop of water given
> Repaid by fresh supplies from Heaven".

During the Victorian period the formal garden frequently revived what was considered a design style. Superb illustration of this are afforded by two country houses built in the New Forest: Brockenhurst Park, where the gardens were considered Italianate and the gardens of Rhinefield House, where they adopted a Jacobean theme; the architectural Jacobean motifs found inside the house being carried on through the balustrading and gateways in the gardens.

At Brockenhurst the gardens were set out in the 1890's for John Morant. The gardens were widely photographed by W.J. Day about 1906;[6] they appeared in Country Life in 1901; in C. Holmes volume on *The Gardens of England in Southern and Western Counties* in 1907, in Jekyll's *Garden Ornament* and were painted by G.S. Elgood.[7] All these show what must have been one of the finest Italianate gardens of the period. Statues and topiary abound; there was a Dutch garden, yew avenues and a broad central canal with urns and steps at the end furthest from the house, which led up to a terrace.

The formal gardens at Rhinefield House are contemporary with those at Brockenhurst. A comprehensive collection of photographs taken during the construction of the house and gardens in the 1890's have made it possible to reconstruct the sequence of the gardens at Rhinefield. Indeed the collection includes some photographs of the gardens at Brockenhurst and feature the visiting Miss Mabel Walker, later Mrs Walker Munro, for whom the gardens and house at Rhinefield were built. The gardens were probably built by the architect of the house Romaine-Walker, who is known to have designed the parterre garden at Luton Hoo; however, no plans for the gardens at Rhinefield are as yet known. The gardens were laid out on a series of terraces with a central canal emphasised by yew hedges and a gravel walk. Flanking the canal nearest to the house were two parterre gardens enclosed by yew hedges. Another topiary garden was set out in the form of a Tudor rose and there was a maze, an open air theatre and croquet lawn.

In complete contrast of size are the formal gardens at Compton End. They were set out from 1895 onwards by a local Winchester architect George Herbert Kitchin (c. 1870-1951). He was a true architect in the Arts and Crafts tradition. Little is known of his early training but by 1903 he had set up practice in Winchester. Kitchin's sketchbooks in the RIBA drawings collection include a sketch of Gertrude Jekyll's Munstead Wood

6. National Monuments Record, Historic Buildings and Monuments Commission.

7. Elgood, G.S., and Jekyll, G., *Some English Gardens*, 1904.

View from balcony, *Rhinefield*

made in August 1901, and he seems to have visited Lutyens in April of that year.[8] From 1895 onwards he united two seventeenth century cottages in Compton End to form his house and started to lay out the gardens. The gardens were written about in *Country Life* and featured on contemporary calendars. The author H. Avray Tipping discussed the garden in his book *The Garden of Today* (1933):

> "even where the Garden of Pleasure is to occupy no more than a quarter of an acre is well exemplified in the garden laid out for his own enjoyment around an old thatched cottage near Winchester by Mr G.H. Kitchin, FRIBA. The plan (end papers) shows that, small as it is, it combines formality with informality. The area being flat and rectangular, the former method plays the larger part . . . south of the central way is a water garden — a lily pool with paved ways and flower beds. From a garden room added to the south end of the cottage we step out along a path formally edged with borders but ending with rough segmental steps taking you down into a slight hollow, shady and tree set . . . which succeeds in giving you some feeling of recluseness despite it measuring only about 10 yards in width and 30 in length".

These gardens unite the formal garden to the cottage garden and achieve a unique quality which persists still.[9]

Despite the reputation that the naturalised English landscape garden achieved, the successful combination of many architectural styles and elements in a formally designed setting is an achievement of almost equal importance.

8. *Architects of the Arts and Crafts Movement.* R.I.B.A. Drawings Series, 1983.
9. Kitchin's other known garden design for extensive formal gardens are at Lyegrove House, Avon which he designed for the Countess of Westmoreland.

The blasted tree.

The New Forest & The Picturesque

MAVIS BATEY

The Revd. William Gilpin, Vicar of Boldre in the New Forest from 1778 until his death in 1804, was the pioneer of the Picturesque, a strange, homebred movement which had far-reaching effects. Picturesque theory sprang from the 18th century obsession with painting. As yet there was no British School of landscape painting and it was the Italian scenery painted by Claude and Poussin, seen on the Grand Tour, which infatuated the Dilettanti. This was all to change when Gilpin promoted the Picturesque Tour of the Homeland in the 1780s. Roads had greatly improved and the search for picturesque beauty in the out-of-the-way regions of Britain soon became a favourite pastime, especially as the Grand Tour had been halted by unrest in Europe. Gilpin's evocative drawings of wild British landscape with ruined fortresses and abbeys were seen as an authentic setting for Gray's Bard, Percy's *Reliques of Ancient English Poetry* and the stories of chivalry and purple abbots which had already fired the imagination of the 1770s.

In everything he saw or read Gilpin called in the painter's eye and this was the basis for his picturesque creed. "By Picturesque", he said, "I mean precisely nothing more than such ideas as can be formed into a picture". He was taught to draw by a gifted soldier father who was garrisoned at Carlisle Castle. He spent part of his life at Scaleby Castle on the Borders, and castles, border warfare and rugged scenery were at the heart of his picturesque imagination. After taking his degree at the Queen's College, Oxford, he was for many years a schoolmaster at Cheam, where he was at pains to cultivate a "picture-making faculty" in his pupils when they read the classics. In 1768 he published an *Essay on Prints* for the instruction of the large new public for whom cheap prints had become available. He showed how to apply the principles of painting to the examination of prints to enable the layman to appreciate such matters as "design, disposition, keeping and the distribution of light".

From studying pictures and cultivating a picture imagination when reading it was a short step for Gilpin to suggest that the traveller should use the same faculty in viewing landscape. In the Cheam school holidays he travelled to out-of-the-way places "in search of picturesque beauty" and, for his own amusement, recorded with descriptions and on-the-spot sketches what he found to be "pencil-provoking" in the Wye Valley, the Highlands, the Lakes and other picturesque regions of Britain. Although these journeys were made in the 1770s it was not until after he had left Cheam and settled in the New Forest that he was persuaded by his friends to publish his Picturesque Tours. They were immediately popular and Gilpin's association of pictures with the appreciation of scenery became a craze. Tourists in search of picturesque beauty would record the scene on the spot in their sketch books or from indicated "stations" view it in their landscape mirrors. A scene not worthy of painting was a mere place and disregarded.

The craze that Gilpin started is best described by the daughter of another Hampshire parson, Jane Austen, who was, according to her brother Henry, at a very early age "enamoured of Gilpin on the Picturesque". The fashionable Tilneys in *Northanger Abbey* were seen to be "viewing the country with the eyes of persons accustomed to painting and deciding on

Left top:
William Gilpin *The Blasted Tree*, Bodleian Library (ms. Eng. misc. e. 498. Fol. 24)

Left bottom:
From Gilpin's *Practical Hints on Landscape Gardening*

41

its capabilities of being formed into pictures" and when Henry Tilney delivers his "lecture on the Picturesque" the young heroine is instructed on "fore-grounds, distances, and second distances — side-screens and perspectives — lights and shades" in true Gilpin style. Like the heroine of *Pride and Prejudice*, Jane Austen studied Gilpin's Northern Tour before setting out on her own tour of the Peak District with her mother and sister in 1806 and made herself conversant with the "face of the country" and its picturesque character:

> "When we do return, it shall not be like other travellers, without being able to give one accurate idea of anything. We will know where we have gone — we will recollect what we have seen. Lakes, mountains, and rivers, shall not be jumbled together in our imaginations".

At the end of their picturesque tour of Derbyshire the Austens went to live in Southampton, where they remained for three years, before settling at Chawton. Writing from Castle Square somewhat disparaging of some neighbours, who had also been travelling, she concluded "nor could I see anything in them of Taste or Feeling that merited them making their late Tour".

Hampshire as a county was not recommended for picturesque travel: it lacked ruggedness, which had come to be seen by the theorists as the essential element of the Picturesque, giving it its own aesthetic category distinct from the Beautiful and the Sublime. William Cobbett called the Austen country around Steventon and Chawton eminently liveable in but it was this fertile domestic quality in its rural landscape that disqualified it from picturesque status. Clearly some of the Austen family endorsed the Cobbett point of view and like Edward Ferrars in *Sense and Sensibility* admired fine scenery, but, to the annoyance of the heroine, not on picturesque principles:

> "I do not like crooked, twisted, blasted trees. I admire them much more if they are tall, straight and flourishing, I do not like ruined, tattered cottages. I am not fond of nettles, or thistles, or heath blossoms. I have more pleasure in a snug farm-house than a watch-tower — and a troop of tidy, happy villages please me better than the finest banditti in the world".

Gilpin passed through Hampshire when making his Western Tour in 1775, but the only scenes he found picturesque, or worthy of painting, were the ruins of Netley Abbey and a distant view of Southampton with its defensive walls across the water. He noted, however, when skirting the New Forest, but unable to stop to investigate, "some of the most inchanting sylvan scenery, that the pencil of nature ever drew". He remembered this two years later when his admirer and former pupil William Mitford of Exbury offered him the living of Boldre and he set off without delay accompanied by his wife, who clearly wished to apply criteria other than the picturesque when making up their minds. Gilpin described this newly-discovered picturesque region enthusiastically to his friend and ally, the Revd. William Mason:

> "Our road led us through the heart of the new forest — such scenes of wood, as I had never beheld. I had often before skirted the new-forest, but never penetrated its depths. For more than a dozen miles we rode past thousands & thousands of ancient oaks, with every one of which a man would wish to form an intimacy; & continued among them, till we knew, by our skill in geography, together with the intimation of mile-

stones, that we were within 2 or 3 miles of the place we aimed at. 'My dear', said I, turning from the trees to my wife, 'I am perfectly satisfyed, & will give the postilion orders to turn back, if you please. To be within the distance of a walk of such scenery as this, is all I desire'. But my wife rather wished to see the house & conveniences. . . so we trudged on to Vicar's hill; which is the name of the place which will probably be our future abode. It is, I assure you, a sweet spot; & there is a view from the parlour-windows, enough to make a man jump out of them. If I have time, I will annex a sketch of it".

The view from Vicar's Hill and along the ridge above Lymington overlooking the Isle of Wight was to compensate Gilpin for the loss of his beloved Lake District, for here in the sea-coast view "the island appearing like a distant range of mountains gives the channel the form of a great lake". The novelty of seabirds in the estuary of the Beaulieu river reminded him of picturesque descriptive passages in Virgil. An embowered castle he had in his own church, which like all the other forest churches was on rising ground in order to be seen by scattered parishioners in the often pathless forest. Having spent his youth in Border castles he wrote with satisfaction that its "imbattled tower among the trees takes the form of a lofty castle".

William Gilpin *Approach to Netley Abbey,* Bodleian Library (ms. Eng. misc. e. 508 Fol.)

The forest scenery all around added a new dimension to his picturesque thinking. After over ten years making a systematic study of the history and topography of the area, the verderers' courts, scenery and animals he finally published in 1791 his detailed observations in *Remarks on Forest Scenery and other Woodland Views (relative chiefly to Picturesque Beauty) illustrated by the Scenes of the New-Forest in Hampshire.* His brother Sawrey drew the forest animals for him. As he said in its Preface, dedicated to his patron William Mitford, one of the Verderers of the New Forest:

"When your friendship fixed me in this pleasing retreat, within the precincts of New-forest, I had little intention of wandering farther among its scenes, than the bounds of my own parish; or of amusing myself any more with writing on picturesque subjects. But one scene drew me on to another; till at length I had traversed the whole forest. The subject was new to me. I had been much among lakes, and mountains; but I had never lived in a forest. I knew little of its scenery. Every thing caught my attention; and as I generally had a memorandum-book in my hand, I made minutes of what I observe".

The Revd. William Gilpin combined parochial duties and picturesque amusement. He visited parishioners in remote parts of the forest sketching and collecting skeleton leaves on the way and noting in his memorandum books the bark, foliage, ramifications and exposed roots of the trees, pools of water, sandy banks and rocky ground. In the same book he would sometimes jot down notes on the weather and thoughts for his next sermon. The close forest scenes delighted him and he felt an affinity with the Dutch painters Swanewelt and Waterlo who:

"penetrated their retreats; and when they found a little opening, or recess, that pleased them, they fixed it on the spot. They studied its various forms — how easily the large boughs parted; and how negligently the smaller were interwoven — how elegantly the foliage hung; and what various shapes its little tuftings exhibited. All these things they observed and copied with exact attention".

He also admired the more savage Salvator Rosa aspects of the trees such as a "blasted oak, ragged, scathed and leafless shooting its peeled, white branches athwart the gathering blackness of some rising storm", which he felt transferred its great ideas to the landscape.

Although Gilpin never himself set out to advise on improving landscape according to principles based on picturesque observation, he was, nevertheless a great influence on the high phase of landscape gardening. After the death of "Capability" Brown in 1783 many so-called Brownian landscape gardeners took what they saw to be his improvement formula of clumped trees, belts, shaven lawns and pieces of water and applied it wherever they were working, regardless of the character of the region. This was frowned upon by the generation that, like Jane Austen's heroines, had acquired a new sense of regionalism from Gilpin. His Picturesque Observations on the Wye (1782); the Lakes (1786); the Highlands (1789) and the New Forest (1791) had taught them to analyse scenery and to observe how differently Nature "works up" landscape in different regions and for them systematised improvement imposed on a region could only be contrary to picturesque taste.

Gilpin's critical remarks on landscape gardening occur mostly in *Remarks on Forest Scenery* since he could countenance nothing but the most judicious improvement in his beloved New Forest; wholesale clearance of forest lawn, artificial water, temples and other works of art were "awkward and disgusting". Although he reserved his judgement on Brown's planting at Paultons he objected to the damming up of the little forest stream and was particularly severe about the owner having thrown a glaring white Chinese bridge across the water. Jane Austen, who had herself made excursions into the New Forest from Southampton, obviously agreed with his comments and when in *Pride and Prejudice* she wanted to show Mr Darcy's impeccable taste she emphasized that at Pemberley his stream had no artificial appearance and the simple bridge across it was quite "in character with the general air of the scene". Elizabeth Bennet whose erstwhile disapproval of the hero was rapidly being overcome in his picturesque grounds "had never seen a place, where natural beauty had been so little counteracted by an awkward taste".

Gilpin did acknowledge, however, that the aristocracy played a vital part in the balance of the ecology of the New Forest. The government of the New Forest was still, with the exception of the abolition of forest law, much as it was when it was created by William the Conqueror. The forest was divided into walks, each of which had a ducal lodge. The lord-warden, then the Duke of Gloucester, had one, and others were owned by the Duke of Bolton and Lord Delaware, who appointed their own forest keepers to preserve their hunting rights. It was in their interest to preserve the trees and the grazing grounds of the deer and hogs which throve on the beech mast. Some lodges such as Rhinefield, once the hunting lodge of Charles II, set in a "vast circle of forest scenery of every species — extensive woods, skirted heaths — intermixtures of wood and lawn" even managed to present their preserves picturesquely and earned Gilpin's praise. The forest grazing lawns had classical overtones as sung by Pope in Windsor Forest:

"There interspers'd with Woods and Verdant Plains
Such as possess'd of old the 'Arcadian Swains"

and, in Gilpin's picturesque eye were vastly to be preferred to the landscape gardeners' lawns:

"What are the lawns of Hagley, or any other place celebrated for this species of artificial landscape, but paltry imitations of the genuine works of Nature?"

Gilpin often admires garden scenes which provide the foreground to picturesque views, however, and in *Remarks on Forest Scenery* he devotes a lot of attention to those, which like his own Vicar's Hill, commanded a view of the Isle of Wight. His neighbour at Walhampton sought only to display extensive views of the Island and the intervening channel which he felt were rather to be called "amusing than picturesque". At Pylewell the owner had managed both the "amusing" extensive view of the busy Solent from his lawn and picturesquely composed views from the woodland walk which encircled the lawn. By means of a cupola on top of the house at D'Oyly (now Newtown) Park really "capital" views had been achieved, not only of the Forest, the Island and the open sea, but eastwards of the sails of the fleet stationed at Spithead, undeniably both amusing and picturesque. The owner was then engaged on replanning the garden scenes to gain the foreground effects seen at Pylewell. Not surprisingly Gilpin commended the way in which William Mitford, after frequent on the spot encouragement, had treated his picturesque woodland rides at Exbury. He particularly admired how at one station his patron had managed to exclude the rest of the Island and by judicious planting frame a picture of Carisbroke Castle on an eminence.

These framed pictures, breaking prospect down into "hide and discover" views, became part of the stock-in-trade of the picturesque landscape gardener. They were used most effectively at Mount Edgcumbe on a Cornish headland overlooking the Tamar estuary, where they were much admired by Mason and Gilpin. William Mason who translated Gilpin's picturesque into gardening ideas gives the method for planting such peephole scenes in his poem "The English Garden":

"Here for a while with cedar or with larch,
That from the ground spread their close texture, hide
The view entire. Then o'er some lowly tuft
Where rose and woodbine bloom, permit its charms
To burst upon the sight; now thro' a copse
Of beech, that rear their smooth and stately trunks,
Admit it partially, and half exclude,
And half reveal its graces; in this path,
How long soe'er the wanderer roves, each step
Shall wake fresh beauties; each short point present
A different picture, new, and yet the same".

Mason was unsuccessful in persuading Gilpin to write a commentary for The English Garden as Gilpin felt his precepts applied only to landscape painting and the picturesque enjoyment of scenery. Mason argued in many heated debates with Gilpin that picturesque principles could be applied to gardening.

"Take thy plastic spade, it is thy pencil
Take thy seeds, thy plants, they are thy colours"

One place where Mason's plastic spade is much in evidence is Nuneham in Oxfordshire. Its owner, Lord Harcourt, who had made it possible for Gilpin's illustrated tours to be published, had tried to outbid Colonel Mitford of Exbury by offering the picturesque parson the living of his church situated in his beautiful landscape garden overlooking the Thames. Gilpin, preferring forest to park scenery declined, presumably before his wife had time to compare the conveniences of the two rectories on offer. William Mason was Lord Harcourt's friend and garden adviser and had already laid out a Gilpin tour overlooking the Thames with distant views of Oxford framed by trees and shrubs. He only worked on a small scale however, and, with a rectory in the North and many requests for gardening advice, he was unable to deal with the thousand acres of unimproved parkland at Nuneham. In 1779 Capability Brown was called in and the two landscape gardeners worked together for several years. Brown enjoyed working for a sensitive and picturesque landowner in preference to the "stare" views he was asked to create for most of his wealthy clients. He made a woodland walk to the South of the house, still called Brown's Walk, which presented vignettes of Thames landscape as Mason had done in a smaller area to the North. The path was bordered with trees and shrubs and sunk in places so that the viewer only had the required occasional glimpses of the river.

Working with Mason at Nuneham on picturesque riverside walks was an experience that stood Brown in good stead when he received a New Forest commission. This work, which was almost his last, was for the landscaping of the Drummond family's cottage orné overlooking the Solent, known as Boarn Hill, now replaced by Cadland House. Brown had already worked for the Hon. Robert Drummond, his banker, at his main house Cadlands, now overtaken by the Fawley Refinery. Gilpin admired Brown's work there, even the clumps which he thought were "just such as the picturesque eye would wish to introduce into the landscape". The views too were presented with admirable effect from grand woody foregrounds. Brown's plan for Boarn Hill, now being restored, shows the sea bank with a gravel path leading through a banked shrubbery, reminscent of "Brown's Walk" at Nuneham. Gilpin had finished most of his manuscript Forest Scenery by 1780 so that he did not have the chance to see at Boarn Hill Brown's "hide and discover" views of the Isle of Wight and shrubbery foreground plantations on the best picturesque principles.

Gilpin directly influenced Regency planting by his remarks that any designer of artificial landscape would do well to study the natural planting of the Forest which furnished endless varieties of form and grouping, projection and recess of woodlands and islands and peninsulas of wild planting on open lawns. William Mason first took this up by suggesting that the garden lawn should imitate the forest lawn with its underwood tufts of thorn and mazy spaces.

"His taste will best conceive
The new arrangement, whose free footsteps, us'd
To forest haunts, have pierc'd their opening dells,
Where frequent tufts of sweetbriar, box, or thorn,
Steal on the greensward, but admit fair space
For many a mossy maze to wind between

At Ditchley, Loudon suggested that exotic trees, shrubs and flowers should be grouped and scattered over the lawn "in the same way that thorns, oaks, hazels and weeds are in the forest", Repton, whose on-the-spot water colours show the influence of Gilpin, spoke of the forest near his Essex home as the source of his landscape inspiration. This was in his Red Book for Claybury, prepared in 1791, the year that Gilpin's Forest Scenery appeared.

Francis Towne, *Netley Abbey*, Southampton City Art Gallery

The mazy spaces of forest lawns were particularly good for forming perambulations in public parks as Nash showed in St James's Park where he used "the same principles that hold good in all wild wood and shrub plantations". Nash even gave the Prince Regent a forest lawn appearance at the Brighton Pavilion.

Gilpin's former pupil, William Sawrey Gilpin, became a professional landscape gardener in the 1820s, developing his uncle's ideas on forest scenery in *Practical Hints on Landscape Gardening*. His Scotney Castle is the best example of what William Gilpin meant by picturesque, "that kind of beauty which would look well in a picture". The Picturesque Movement pioneered by a shy Hampshire parson exerted a great influence on art, architecture, literature and landscape gardening, and because it taught whole generations a visual appreciation of landscape it is still felt in rural planning and on societies connected with the protection of landscape.

ARCHIVE SOURCES
for Hampshire Gardens

ROSEMARY DUNHILL

Over the last decade there has been an increasing realisation by such groups as archaeologists and architectural historians that a study of documentary sources can greatly enrich a study on the ground. The same is true in the area of garden history; visual or archaeological evidence can be supplemented and explained by documentary evidence. In the case of great estates, detailed plans, reports and accounts may provide a readily understandable picture of developments. In other cases, little or nothing may survive with direct bearing on the garden being studied. In such circumstances it can be valuable to look at surviving documentation for a similar garden — or a garden of a similar period — and to learn from this.

Some items of relevance exist for all or most of the county, but the key to finding out what sources survive for an individual property usually lies in the ownership of the property. Printed works such as the *Victoria County History* (available in the County and City Record Offices[1] and in the reference departments of the larger libraries within the county) will provide the information for larger properties. From the mid 19th century trade and post office directories show the occupancy of substantial houses. It is worth remembering that properties, including large houses, were frequently leased, and relevant details may be found among the papers of the family to whom the lease was made, as well as those of the owners. For smaller properties also there is a range of original records which can help to establish the chain of ownership: electoral registers, rate books, tithe apportionments, taxation records, supplementing the most obvious source, title deeds, where these have survived. (The title deeds, of course, will normally be with the family records which the object of this exercise is to trace.) Staff at the record offices will advise on the availability and use of these sources or recommend relevant publications.

When the ownership is known, steps can be taken to establish whether records of that family — or families — have survived. The local record offices will be able to indicate whether they hold the records among their deposits, and if not may be willing to make enquiries to see if they survive elsewhere in the county. In Hampshire the County Record Office and the Gardens Trust have co-operated over a number of such enquiries, and additional collections have been deposited in the record office as a result. The recently established Hampshire Archives Trust has a particular interest in locating and surveying records held privately within the county and advising on their storage and conservation. Enquiries can also be made of the National Register of Archives[2], which maintains an index to collections of archives in repositories, and some in private hands, throughout the country. Material will not necessarily be located in the county where the property is situated; the property may have formed part of a large estate based in another county.

One class of record likely to survive in some form for most properties is maps. An excellent starting point for studying any garden earlier than the last quarter of the 19th century is the first edition of the 25 inch to the mile ordnance survey maps, published about 1870, with a high degree of accurate detail; there is a good, though not complete, series in the County

1. Hampshire has three local authority record offices: Hampshire Record Office, 20 Southgate Street, Winchester SO23 9EF; Portsmouth City Records Office, 3 Museum Road, Portsmouth PO1 2LE; Southampton City Record Office, Civic Centre, Southampton SO9 4XL. The documents whose references are quoted below are all in Hampshire Record Office. Details about the Hampshire Archives Trust can be obtained from Hampshire Record Office.
2. Quality Court, Chancery Lane, London WC2A 1HP.

48

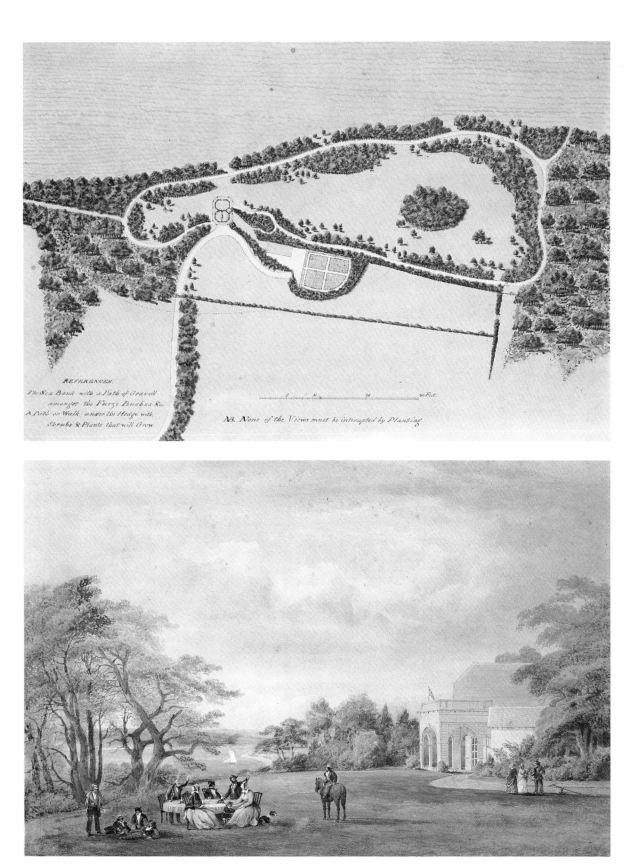

Mottisfont, Heather Angel

Bramdean, Heather Angel

Record Office, and the City Record Offices and larger libraries have series covering their areas. Most parts of the county are also covered either by the tithe maps of the late 1830s/early 1840s, which show every building and plot of land except where tithe had already been commuted for a fixed rent charge, or by the late 18th/early 19th century inclosure maps which often included provision for commuting tithes. Private estate maps may survive to push the picture further back and can be full of interesting detail, often showing buildings and other features in three dimensional form, but there is no county-wide series of these; they were drawn up to meet the needs and at the expense of the local landowner and normally survive as part of his records. A particularly fine example in Hampshire which has been used by the Gardens Trust to draw up restoration plans in conjunction with the owner is that of the Tylney Hall estate, Rotherwick, dated 1774. Another charming example, unfortunately badly faded, shows the house and gardens of William Heighes of East Anstey near Alton in 1731, with not only the individual trees, distinguishing between the varieties, but each brick in the wall showing.[3]

Records in pictorial form are another obvious source. Photographs are of course comparatively recent, but can throw unparalleled light on gardens from the late 19th century; the marvellous series depicting the development of the gardens at Rhinefield House, near Brockenhurst, in the restoration of which the Gardens Trust is also involved, spring readily to mind. Sale particulars for larger houses often include photographs of parts of the garden, and sometimes also descriptions and even layout plans. For example, the 1895 sale catalogue for Heckfield Place, home of Lord Eversley, former Speaker, describes the gardens and pleasure grounds as "having received the special care and attention of the late noble owner, who devoted years of his life in forming them and spared no expense in bringing them to their present state of perfection." Items described include a broad terrace walk, lofty orangery, Italian garden, sloping velvety lawn, two ornamental lakes, rustic summer house, pinetum, broad expanse of lawn studded with named trees, two aviaries, an ice house, and two extensive fruit and kitchen gardens. In the pre-photograph period prints and drawings were made of most properties with any pretensions to stateliness, and though rarely concentrating specifically on the garden at least usually show the house in its setting. Those which show gardens in Hampshire in the greatest detail are Johannes Kip's early 18th century print of Southwick, seemingly taken from a static balloon, and a print of Pylewell House near Lymington, similar in style though less detailed, by an unknown artist.[4]

To turn now to the records which may survive in family and estate collections, the most immediately relevant are plans, accounts and correspondence. All are in evidence in one of the finest collections in the Hampshire Record Office, the Jervoise of Herriard archive. The Jervoises appear to have thrown practically nothing away, and the very bulk of the surviving records has proved a bar to easy access, but recent work by Mrs. Sally Jeffery on the extensive series of plans to the house and gardens and related material in the accounts has greatly aided research by others.[5] The gardens were newly laid out in the late 17th/early 18th century after a series of plans dating from 1699; there is a particularly interesting rough free-hand plan by the owner Thomas Jervoise himself which Mrs. Jeffery considers may best represent the work actually carried out at this time. Also in

3. 10M48/1; 4M51/451.
4. 38M49/7/191; 15M84 P3/666; 15M84 P3/82.
5. Jeffrey, Sally, "John James and George London at Herriard: architectural drawings in the Jervoise of Herriard collection", *Architectural History* vol. 28 (1985).

Jervoise's hand is a rough sketch showing the view-lines from the east end of his new house. An account book for 1699 includes references to work in "the new garden", and lengthy bills for the purchase of plants and seed date from this period. One dated 18 January 1699/1700 comprises 34 items, all but five different types of seed, including "orang Carrott", "Read Carrot", "London Leeke", "best Cabbeg Lettis", "Seleshe Lettis", "Cost Lettis", "Cowcumber", "London Readish", "Winser Beanes", and "nursstushin". A slightly later list headed "the Accounte of seeds wanting at Heriard for the yeare 1708" includes African and French marigolds and "small yalow Lupens sensible & humble plantes". Back in 1699/1700 there is also a list of over 40 different types of fruit tree which apparently relate to a planting plan. Many of the plants and trees supplied at Herriard at this time came from the nursery of George London and Henry Wise at Brompton in London.[6]

Plan of Herriard Gardens, John Pearce of Upton Grey, 1818. (44M69 P1/75) Hampshire Record Office.

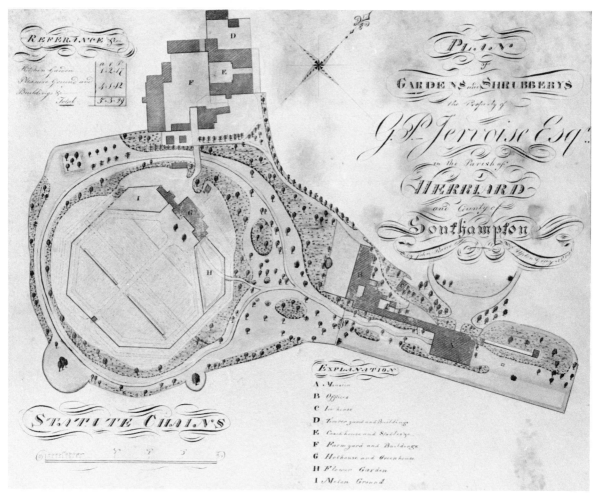

This collection also includes letters to Thomas Jervoise from his agent Thomas Austin and from various nurserymen from as early as 1694. Several relate to the purchase of large numbers of fir trees and show Jervoise's concern for a good bargain and insistence that his agent should shop around. Others relate to staffing problems. Austin writes regretfully in 1694:

"Eversince I gave the Gardner notice to provide himselfe a service he has bin dilligent to excesse & is one of the first up in the house. . . Had

6.   44M69 P1/65-6; 44M69 E19.

not the other bin ordered to come I wish wee had tryd him farther." Five years later there is a letter from the gardener himself, in a surprisingly literate script, asking to be discharged at the end of the year "by reason of my indisposition and unhealthiness of Body".[7]

The gardens at Herriard were substantially remodelled at the end of the 18th century. Repton was consulted and payments for his visits are recorded in the accounts. The Jervoise of the day, George Purefoy, showed a similar personal interest to his predecessor Thomas. In 1802 he surveyed the gardens with Capt. Monro and recorded his measurements. In 1796, when the first brick of the new garden wall was laid, the names and occupations of all the workmen present were listed and five shillings was distributed among the men. There are further detailed accounts; one, with the nurseryman John Armstrong of North Warnborough, covers the period December 1794 to November 1797 and comprises 13 long and closely written pages, totalling £171.17s.6d.[8]

Another, though much smaller collection where the development of gardens is illustrated by a good series of accounts is that relating to the Dumaresq family of Pelham Place, Newton Valence. The garden was laid out soon after the completion of the house, in the 1780s. In 1782, 16,000 bricks were carried from West Meon to build the garden wall; the cost of the building was £89. The following year 3000 quicksets were purchased, and the orchard was stocked with dwarf and standard peaches and nectarines, damsons, plums, cherries, apples, medlars and pears. £2.16s. was paid for the carting of "mold" from the turnpike road to manure the garden, and in 1784, along with estimates for a water closet and a new larder, Thomas Dumaresq received an estimate of £14.15s.5d. for a "Green House Leeving oute the Brickwork". Fifty years later William Dumaresq spent over £200 on the erection of a new green house, to be heated with hot water, and the addition of a hot water heating system to the old green house. He also invested in large quantities of trellis.[9]

But one of the most interesting items in this collection is an illustrated description of a hot bed and frame similar to a melon frame but to be used for growing vines, headed "Directions from Mr. Knight's Gardiner at Downton". Richard Payne Knight, the author of *An Analytical Inquiry into the Principles of Taste*, was one of the foremost exponents of the picturesque movement in architecture and landscape, and built a castle at Downton in Herefordshire between 1772 and 1778 in illustration. It is fascinating to see his influence exercised here not through the printed word but through the friendly interchange of gardening tips. Similarly among the Calthorpe papers, which include extensive early 19th century correspondence, there are two descriptions of ice houses, presumably requested with a view to providing one at Elvetham. The first, written from Birmingham by Calthorpe's agent John Harris in 1823, describes and illustrates the ice house at Packington, built with several others by E. Eele at a cost of 10 guineas excluding materials. In 1826 Calthorpe received another letter on the same subject, describing the ice house at Elmdon, Warwickshire, where the writer, A.L. Lillingstone, tells him:

"I have destroyed the expensive entrance which was made to that at Elmdon as being detrimental and at variance with philosophical principles."

These letters form a reminder that information may turn up in unlikely places. What we have in Hampshire is the letters received by Calthorpe;

7.   44M69 E19.
8.   44M69 E21.
9.   4M52/220-3, 234-5.

The Curtis Family in their Garden, 1860s,
Hampshire County Museums Service

the letters he wrote, perhaps in his turn describing innovations at Elvetham, may well be in collections in other county record offices.[10]

Ice houses also figure in the records of another well-documented garden, that of Broadlands. A paper of 1823, endorsed "Directions for making a cheap Ice House", ignores philosophical principles in favour of the severely practical, concluding: "Should Rats infest the House, a wire case will be necessary". The Broadlands archive includes the most detailed planting plans I have seen, one of the late 18th century listing 131 trees and marking their precise position in the kitchen garden. Another treasure is a letter from Capability Brown, describing the work he carried out at Broadlands between 1766 and 1779 and "with an unfeigned heart" thanking his patron "for numberless Civilities, kind usage and pleasant imployment". In 1797 the gardener Knight wrote an account to Lord Palmerston of a half hour visit paid by the Prince of Wittenburg to the house and grounds, and the chicken, ham, beef, craw fish, butter, oranges, sweet cakes, madeira, lisbon, sherry, and port wines provided for his refreshment. At the end of 1807 the Viscount listed what he had achieved in the grounds during the year: the completion of the rebuilding of the park wall, which had collapsed after the first attempt; the rerouting of the footpath through the park, the repair of the hothouses; the thinning of the clumps and plantations; last but not least the sacking of the above-mentioned Knight, who "had behaved excessively ill. . . He not only totally neglected the kitchen garden & pleasure grounds at Broadlands but plundered them of many valuable trees and shrubs, carried away flag stones, dung etc. for himself and his friends."[11]

The records of the Sloane Stanley estate at Paultons near Romsey contain nothing about the laying out and stocking of the garden, but they do document very clearly the building of one of the most distinctive features of the grounds there, the bridge. Among the papers are water colour drawings (1828) showing two alternative designs by the architect C.H. Tatham, who had been employed by Sloane Stanley on the house. Tatham also sent an estimate for building the bridge, to which he received a crusty reply that Sloane Stanley intended to build the bridge with his own workmen, paying Tatham only for the plans and drawings. Correspondence with the Cardiff Iron Foundry, who produced the parts and shipped them to Eling Quay with a man to assemble them, shows the owner continuing to take a strong personal interest and constantly querying costs.[12]

This strong personal involvement of the owner in the development of his garden seems to be the keynote in most of the surviving documentary evidence. The professional gardener is usually a more shadowy figure, though the examples quoted above show that the documents do bring him too into the foreground from time to time. Light is sometimes thrown by their wills and inventories. Francis Penbrooke of Binsted, for example, who died in 1641, seems to have been quite comfortably off, including among his possessions "3 spitting shovells, 2 irone Rakes, 4 pronges, & other garninge (i.e. gardening) tooles", valued at 7s.6d. Daniel Beamont of Netley in 1652 had two hoes ("houghs"), a spade, and a pair of shears. It is of course very interesing to know what tools gardeners had at their disposal. Prints and drawings were mentioned earlier, and there is a particularly fine one of the Warden's garden at Winchester College taken from a drawing by J. Buckler and printed between 1822 and 1839, which shows a wheelbarrow and garden roller. For a period more recent still, the County Record Office

10. 4M52/232; 26M62F/C624, C978.
11. 27M60/103/26; 27M60/103/18/3,7,8,19.
12. 28M57/73/1-10.

The Warden's Garden at Winchester College J. Buckler, c. 1830 (15M84 P3/797) Hampshire Record Office.

holds some of the records of the Hillier family, gardeners for three generations. They include notebooks reflecting the training of gardeners in the mid 19th century, with lists of work carried out each day in the great gardens where they served, including Sion Park at Isleworth and Studeley Royal in Yorkshire. There are letters to Edwin Hillier from horticulturalists the world over, exchanging information, cuttings and seeds. There are also a range of the firm's catalogues, showing what was available locally to Hampshire gardeners.[13]

Most of the records I have quoted above relate to the creation and development of gardens. I end with one which shows the creator's enjoyment. The original is not in Hampshire, but in the archives at Kew; it is a letter written by Thomas Garnier, Vicar of Bishopstoke and Dean of Winchester to Sir William Hooker at Kew. He describes the first flowering of his *Escalonia floribunda* and its immediate attraction of the Admiral butterfly:

"I do not believe that there is another plant of the same kind in Hampshire. . . and say those who best can tell what it is that directs this tribe of insects to discover this plant the very first moment it comes into flower and to revel upon it when not a single one of the same species was to be found upon any other flower in my garden during the whole summer and autumn."

13. 1641B37/1-2; 1652Ad4/1; 15M84 P3/797; 136M82/2, 20-2, 33-4.

A HERMITAGE FOR CADLAND
"afaver as never yet was nown"

NIGEL TEMPLE

By the third quarter of the eighteenth century, hermitages, though not obligatory, were common enough ornaments in fashionable English gardens. These melancholy structures might possess architectural quality, or be formed by adapting natural features that presented themselves in suitably gloomy locations. Hermitages included in their range sophisticated root houses — like the one designed by Thomas Wright at Badminton — and subterranean apartments. One near Preston, Lancashire, was fitted up with a cold bath and chamber organ. At Painshill Park, Surrey, Charles Hamilton constructed a neat octagonal cabin with conical thatched roof on top of a contrived nest of shattered and sawn-off tree trunks,[1] while in the deep ravine at Downton Castle, the seat of Richard Payne Knight, a hermit's cave — probably a natural opening aided by the hand of man — opened in a cliff wall alongside the river Teme.

Really enterprising hermitage owners might install a hired recluse, or possibly acquire a suitable volunteer rent free. By these means a proprietor need never have to inhabit the wretched place himself, yet would possess a remarkable and animated decoration in what might otherwise have been an unattractive backwater of his estate. The Root House at Brocklesby, Lincolnshire, is said to have been inhabited, and the splendid, but sadly lamented Sanctuary at Burley on the Hill, Leicestershire, boasted a named incumbent — Hermit Finch, though Barbara Jones suggests that as the one-time owners were named Finch, this could be a parallel case to Castle Howard.[2] In default of the real thing a fanatical hermitage builder might install a motionless effigy, as at Hawkstone, where Sir Richard Hill had "maintained" a poor man during the day for fourteen years, but "the popular voice against such *slavery* had induced the worthy baronet to withdraw the reality and substitute the figure".[3] By 1810 he had gone. While this hermit's long term of service holding an hourglass and wearing an old goat's beard must have seemed to him an eternity, it did at least earn him immortality of a kind:

"Secluded from the world he lives,
A world of guilt and sin,
   And values, what *it* never gives,
A state of peace within. . .

He warns mankind to turn from *Sin*
Its gilded baits to fly;
Calls them to seriousness within,
And bids them learn to die".

The poet continues his moral reflections less than totally convinced:

"Though thoughts like these impress the mind,
Whilst in the HERMIT'S Cell,
May we not better moments find,
As socially we dwell?"[4]

And by 1830, that self-same 'reality', had dwelt sufficiently socially to have become editor of a magazine.[5]

Hill's effigy was stuffed; others might be of wax. Even more ingenious would have been the construction of a bearded, head-nodding, finger-

1. Bodleian; Gough Maps 30f of 59B "The Hermitage at Painshill after a Drawing of Mr Skell".
2. Jones, Barbara, *Follies and Grottoes*, Constable, 1974: pp. 176-193, "The Hermitages".
3. Timbs, John, *English Eccentrics and Eccentricities*, Bentley, 1866, i, p. 163
4. Salmon, J.W., *The Beauties of Hawkstone Park*, 1817 (3rd edn.).
5. Timbs, *op. cit.* i, p. 162. See *Blackwood's Magazine*, April, 1830, under Noctes Ambrosianae.

S.H. Grimm, *The Hermitage, Selborne*, Courtauld Institute of Art

William Wrighte, Title page from Grotesque Architecture, 1767

Engraving from Roret, 1835/1840

pointing, Bible-reading automaton to entertain one's flagging guests when touring the grounds before dinner.

Numerous other hermitages, some of their more eccentric creators, and an engaging variety of hoary, poetic, philosophical, fugitive, or simply benignly decorative recluses are well recorded in print.[6] While a few further examples will be cited here in passing, our principal purpose is to introduce a unique eremitical document that has recently come to light, and briefly to outline a broader, and a more parochial context for it. But before considering this illustrated letter, it should be noted that in England the popularity of purely ornamental or mood-provoking hermitages as modish garden structures dates from as late as the mid-eighteenth century, and that the rage thereafter might well have gained much impetus from royal example at what we know to day as Kew Gardens.

There were two structures built at Richmond, Surrey, for Queen Caroline, both designed by William Kent. The first, called The Hermitage, was constructed in 1731, but with its rather grand and formal domed Palladian interior is unlikely to have evoked even a spuriously spiritual atmosphere. The architect's second attempt — Merlin's Cave — built four years later, was nearer the mark, as can be judged from John Vardy's cross-sectional drawing in *Some Designs of Mr. Inigo Jones and Mr. Wm. Kent* (1744). This exposes a rustic-Gothick interior, its expansive groined roof being supported by tree trunk columns, while a veritable wild garden of deciduous trees and conifers grows on top. Merlin's Cave was distinguished by six permanent residents, including Minvera, Queen Elizabeth and a wizard — a bizarre assortment, all made of wax. The saga of Stephen Duck, rustic poet, is a tale in itself. Duck, once a farm worker, had a gift with words. He became Keeper of the Queen's hermetic retreats, the Governor of Duck Island, Royal Thatcher, and was sometime rector of Byfleet. He contributed verse to the *Gentleman's Magazine* and a poetic essay On the Queen's Grotto, which appeared in December, 1732:

". . . Now blush, *Calypso*, 'tis but just to yield,
That all your Mossy Caves are here excell'd.
See how the Walls in humble Form advance,
With careless Pride, and simple Elegance,
See Art and Nature strive with equal Grace,
And Fancy charm'd with what she can't surpass. . ."

But in landscaping the royal gardens, Lancelot Brown swept away Kent's work, a point not missed by an anonymous poet (William Mason) when writing *An Heroic Epistle* (1773) against William Chambers' *Dissertation on Oriental Gardening* of the previous year. Chambers, who had by then constructed his Chinese buildings at Kew, ridiculed Brown. Mason's *Epistle* alludes to Merlin's Cave, Duck and Brown in the course of his one hundred and forty-six lines of satirical verse thus:

". . . Come then, prolific Art, and with thee bring
The charms that rise from thy exhaustless spring;
To Richmond come, for see, untutor'd Brown
Destroys those wonders which were once thy own.
Lo, from his melon-ground the peasant slave
Has rudely rush'd, and levell'd Merlin's Cave;
Kock'd down the waxen Wizzard, seiz'd his wand,
Transform'd to lawn what late was Fairy land;

6.   Timbs, *op. cit.*; Jones, *op. cit.*; Festing, S., "Notes and Queries: Amateur and Professional Hermits", *Garden History Society: Newsletter 14*, Summer 1985, pp. 4-6: Also *Newsletter 15*, Autumn 1985: Sitwell, Edith, *English Eccentrics*, Faber & Faber, 1933, Penguin, 1971, and others. See also Hunt, John Dixon, *The Figure in the Landscape*, John Hopkins University Press, 1976.

And marr'd, with impious hand, each sweet design
Of Stephen Duck, and good Queen Caroline. . ."[7]

For that minority who hankered after a life of solitude and austerity combined with a fair measure of independence and freedom, these must have been the golden years. Not only might a purpose-built cell of some pretension set in a princely garden be the prize, but there was the possibility also of food from the employer's table, the opportunity for anonymity or exhibitionism, and probably a wage as well; and not necessarily a pittance either (if one could face up to the challenge for seven years). Such was the case at Painshill. Although no one appears ever to have seen the document (if document there ever was: "advertisement" could, of course, have been broadcast by word of mouth), it has frequently been claimed that Mr. Hamilton advertised for his hermit on the following conditions of employment. He (no hermitesses have been encountered):

"should be provided with a Bible, optical glasses, a mat for his bed, a hassock for his pillow, an hour-glass for his time piece, water for his beverage, food from the house, but never to exchange a syllable with the servant."

The Painshill recluse was required "to wear a camlet robe, never to cut his beard or nails, nor ever stray beyond the limits of the grounds."[8] But the real test was duration, for on breach of any one of the conditions the successful candidate would forfeit the whole of his final reward — seven hundred guineas — a handsome sum but one to be paid only after seven years of such impeccable service. Tradition has it that the appointed hermit lasted but three weeks before being caught at the local inn.

Richard Graves, in his novel *Columella, or the Distres't Anchorite* (1779), relates events at an interview. The hermit "a very venerable figure, with a long white beard, a bald head, and dressed in a long brown cloak almost down to his ankles", had two sticks forming a cross, and a string of peas for a rosary. He claimed already to have served four years in the required capacity elsewhere, but that on the death of his employer, his heir insisted that the hermit should do more work than had originally been agreed, "which was to keep his hermitage clean, and to sit at the door with a book in his hand when any company came". Christopher Hussey adds that it subsequently transpired that the hermit had been sacked "for certain inappropriate relations with a dairymaid", and for being caught with a pipe and ale instead of book and beads.[9]

As well as being advertised for, potential hermits sometimes announced their availability publicly and privately. A letter, sent anonymously to the owner of a Hampshire estate, is the focus of the present account.

Both Henry Holland, the architect, and Lancelot Brown, the improver, were customers of Drummond's Bank, at Charing Cross, London. The Hon. Robert Drummond (1728-1804) became Governor in 1769 and bought Cadland Manor, on the west bank of the Solent, in 1772, as a quiet retreat from London business life. But Drummond was disinclined to do things by halves. Four years later he engaged his two distinguished professional clients to build a new mansion and landscape the grounds. He also bought additional land, including a water-side site at Boarn Hill — on which he built a fishing lodge known as "The Cottage". We gain an insight into Drummond's character on learning that he drew not only freely, but excessively, on his bank's funds (to the tune of a "net incumbrance" of £86,000 on his death), and a glimpse of his life style on reading of what

7. *An Heroic Epistle to Sir William Chambers, Knight,* Almon, 1772 (6th edn.).
8. Timbs, *op. cit.,* p. 157.
9. Hussey, Christopher, *The Picturesque: Studies in a Point of View,* Putnam, 1927, pp. 131-132.

began as an everyday social event at "The Cottage". On Thursday, 7th July, 1785, "A party of gentlemen were assembled to dinner there, when, about three o'clock, smoke was observed to issue from the building, and in less than an hour it was consumed". The furniture having been saved, and Mr. Drummond having for some time disappeared (but to emerge from the smoking pile with the contents of his cellar), "the company sat down. . . to a fine haunch of venison, and the remains of the dinner, and some excellent wines. . ."[10] The rebuilt cottage was burnt down again in 1916 and the present Cadland House built on its site in 1934. Restoration of Brown's garden surrounding it was started in 1983 by Robert Drummond's descendants. He, Robert, was the intended recipient of the anonymous, undated letter, which bore no sender's address, but the superinscription "Directed to the Honble Esqr Drummond Cadland Near Southampton",[11] which direction has been transcribed inside the folded cover in another hand.

The drawing, on the same sheet, shows a primitive visualisation of the hermit's intended abode, with an entrance to the left of the encircling wall and a place for depositing food and drink at the bottom left of the hut itself. So here we have an apparently genuine application for patronage "as never yet was nown", with a first-hand design conceived at grass roots level. What is more, the hopeful recluse stipulated his own conditions of employment, did not anticipate any written or verbal reply from Mr. Drummond, but did expect action on his part — "the soner the Better". The growth of nails, beard and hair, and a seven year stint, were almost statutory job specification clauses. However, the Cadland postulant, unlike Mr. Lawrence, did not even hint of payment, or express any religious intent or pretension: no crossed sticks rudely fixed with nails, no strings of dried peas, no Bible and no monk's robes are mentioned. So if Robert Drummond, whose extensive landscaping and building activities must have been widely known, had put it about — "advertised" — that he would welcome a decorative hermit in his grounds, he might well have been disappointed on this occasion. While, typically, the site should be secluded, a high wall was to be built around the hut, and its occupant would wish to see no one — not even a servant bringing from the house nearby the necessities of life — for the full term of seven years. And as one stated purpose of the retreat was "to se what Nature would turn to in that time", the intended confinement would presumably have been a novel departure for at least this applicant. He does not appear to have been an exhibitionist in the accepted sense, but as our earlier examples have already illustrated, even hermits are apt to yield to temptation.

So far as the hermitage itself is concerned, the drawing is primitive in its handling, rudimentary in its architectural styling, crude in its detailing, and ill-formed in its lettered instructions "round the clock". However, once the main verticals and horizontals had been ruled, spontaneity took over to produce an undeniable charm. The required plan was a square. Beyond that, roof, floor and three elevations were up to Mr. Drummond and his builder, who might have used sliced tree trunks (lapped back to back), hazel rods, branches, or roots in constructing the thatched, tiled, or shingled hut. The floor might be of earth, perhaps with sheep's knuckle bones hammered in like nails, be inlaid with pebbles or shells, or have sawn-off stakes banged in vertically to give a mosaic-like effect. Bark or moss might line the walls, for all of these methods were commonly recommended.

10. *Morning Chronicle, and London Advertiser* Tuesday 12 July, 1785.
11. Cadland House, Drummond Archives.

I have tacking this fredom to aquaint
your honnor it is to ask afaver as never
yet was nown for human Cind to do
that if your honnor pleases to Buld
asmall hut ashermetage Near your
honers house in awood with ahigh
wall round It your honer might hear
of aman to Live in it for 7 years
with out seing any human Creature
that is to se what Nature would turn to
in that time I mean not to Cut my
hair nor yet my Beard nor my Nayls
in that time I shud wish to have all
Neseres of Life Brought to me in
aprivat plase without seing any Body
and if your honner will Give proper
encoredgment for them years I would
[I am Iwill *deleted*] Be at your honners
Servise dirictley
the soner the Better
I have not disskribed my Name hear
to your honnor but I shall hear when
it gose on and I hope then to troble your
honer with a feawe Lines for anser
God Bles you [r?]

(inscribed on drawing, around the hut, from top left)

It might be don / in afortirnight
it might / be built with with [*sic*] old wood
the house / 15 fet Square

(inscribed bottom left on drawing of hut)

private / place

(inscribed on drawing of gate in wall)

[?]

(endorsed in another hand)

Directed to the Honble Esqr Drummond /
Cadland / Near Southampton

Manuscript letter and sketch of Hermitage, The Cadland Trustees

No close precedent for the elevational drawing has been found in a pattern book, though that is hardly surprising: it is a commonplace arrangement. Its design might have been carefully thought out, but the hand that drew it incompetent. Otherwise, any half-remembered or well known church or porch could have provided a point of departure. However, a Gothic chapel design depicted in the sixth edition of a French pattern book, L.E. Audot's *Traité de la Composition et de L'Ornement des Jardins* (1859) bears a general resemblance (Fig. 3) and an undated (c. 1834-40) work, *Encyclopédie-Roret: Manuel de l'Architecte des Jardins*, has a hermitage design closely related to Audot's, but thatched and more rustic. It will be shown that both of these authors published some designs derived from English originals.

Britain had been greatly influenced by Italian, French and Dutch garden design, a fact almost as well known as the wave which was to wash back from these shores and transform the formality of many European gardens into more naturalistic scenes. Hand in hand with this broader movement was detailing, such as the design of suitable garden buildings. To this end numerous examples from English pattern books were published abroad, and some were actually built.

In the context of the Cadland drawing, it would then be instructive to follow the course of judge one pattern book design over the period of a century, bearing in mind its Continental ancestry, and noting later popular debasement of the rustic hermitage image to the level available to every suburban house owner.

William Wrighte's *Grotesque Architecture; or, Rural Amusement* first appeared in 1767. His plate 4 displays an "Oriental Hermitage", a rugged structure, the conical Chinese thatched roof of which is supported by a living tree which penetrates the apex to sprout decoratively above the roof (Fig. 5). Outside, tree trunks support the eaves and flank a rusticated door, above which is a tablet inscribed, it is claimed, in Arabic. The main structure is contained by seats set in irregular alcoves, to be constructed of large rough stones and roots of pollard trees cemented together. The shelter was to be lined with billet wood and moss.

George Louis Le Rouge was a prolific Parisian publisher of maps and engravings. His folio *Detail des Nouveaux Jardins à la Mode (Jardins Anglo-Chinois)* ran to twenty-one handsome cahiers between 1776 and 1787. C 4 (1776) reproduces Wrighte's "Oriental Hermitage" — but the whole image is printed left to right; even the inscription is in reverse. It is as though La Rouge transferred Wrighte's print down onto his copper plate in order to re-engrave it. As a subtitle to his own pattern book, Le Route added "Grottes Et Hermitages/pour les jardins Anglais" (Fig. 6).

We can pick up the trail again in Roret's *Manuel* (c. 1835-40). Plate 108 (Fig. 7) shows the same "Ermitage" design again, but the living tree has gone and its crowning decoration been replaced by a lantern and cruciform finial. The flanking seats have disappeared and the tablet bears in illegible inscription. The last evolutionary phase to be found to date is in Audot's book of 1851. Plate 94 ('Chaumieries') is of the same design again (placed alongside another of Wrighte's pirated inventions). This also lacks seats, and the tree has been removed as a roof support to stand to the left, behind the hut. Now the ex"Arabic" text reads "Nec Plus/Nec Minus".[12]

By 1810 James Pilton's factory was in the King's Private Road, Chelsea. His splendidly engraved letter heading, topped by the royal arms, is

12. The writer has been unable to locate an early edition of Audot's book. If the illustrations referred to were also in these, they might prove to pre-date the Roret designs referred to. To judge from these images alone, this could well be the case, the tree in one case standing aside and behind the hermitage. In the other, it has gone. In the Roret version the 'Arabic' inscription has changed to two lines of Latin: in Audot's version there are two lines — illegible — though the illustration is smaller.

inscribed "established under the distinguished patronage of their Majesties and Royal Family". Pilton manufactured an amazing range of gates, conservatories, menageries, alcoves, venison safes, ornamental dairies and summer retreats. An engraving shows his menagerie, in the near corner of which stands a cylindrical, vermiculated hut with a conical thatched roof (Fig. 9): a garden shelter of some sort that would have been very much at home on the pages of Wrighte's *Grotesque Architecture*. But a close counterpart of Pilton's design does appear in Roret under "Cabanes du Jardin des plantes", and two more variations of it are offered by Audot, one a cabane, the other a pavillon rustique.

What had once been the objects of princely extravagance were now on the brink of being take-away merchandise — no doubt still very well done and with the underpinning guarantee of royal patronage. By the 1900's the process had been completed. Coopers, of the Old Kent Road, would supply a prefabricated "Portable 3-gabled Thatched-Roof Rustic Summer House, No. 306" — "a charming adornment to a garden wherever erected", complete on rail, at their works for £42, while in Paul Hasluck's *Rustic Carpentry* (1911), price one shilling, are do-it-yourself instructions for building an "Octagonal Summer-House with Three Gables", from scratch (with linoleum-covered floor).

To return, finally, to the Cadland hermit's letter: while there is no evidence to suggest that the application is other than by a genuine would-be hermit, we cannot take it for granted that it was in the applicant's own hand. Neither can the possibility that the letter was a sophisticated joke yet be dismissed. Experts date the paper as eighteenth century and the letter has been pasted into an early nineteenth-century commonplace book kept by Robert's son, Andrew Berkeley Drummond (1755-1833). Robert Drummond was a son of William, the fourth Viscount of Strathallan, and the only "Honourable" owner of Cadland. As he died in 1804 it can be taken that the letter was not written later than January 19 of that year. There is no evidence yet that the hermitage was built, but one based on the drawing may stand near the new Cadland House before the end of 1987.

Acknowledgements to Mr. & Mrs. Maldwin Drummond, Linden Huddlestone and Margot Lutze.

"DAM THE FLOWER POTS"
Early Difficulties of Importing Plants by Sea

MALDWIN DRUMMOND

The Royal Navy played a central part in early plant transportation and Portsmouth was the most important port for expeditions and introductions outside London.

The founder of the School of Nautical Studies at Warsash, the late Captain Whalley Wakeford, used to delight in explaining in a sentence, the difference between the Royal Navy and the merchant service.

"The Royal Navy," he said, "were always practicing something they would seldom if ever, be called on to do, while the merchant service was always doing what it never had time to practice".

It is almost certain, though, that the Navy never "practiced" plant collecting, even though from time to time sailors and ships were heavily engaged in the activity. It is difficult in modern terms to picture a Chief Petty Officer with his band of "matelots" in front, starting off his lecture with "What we are going on with now is plant collecting", yet the Admiralty has provided page on page of directions for officers in His or Her Majesty's Navy to aid them to use their time, in far flung ports, for scientific observation. In the first edition, 1849, of A *Manual of Scientific Inquiry* edited by Sir John Herschel and published by John Murray, on the authority of the Lords Commissioners of the Admiralty, the latter wrote collectively:

"It is the opinion of the Lords Commissioners of the Admiralty that it would be to the honour and advantage of the Navy, and conduce to the general interests of Science, if new facilities and encouragement were given to the collection of information upon scientific subjects by the officers, and more particularly by the medical officers, of Her Majesty's Navy, when upon foreign service; and their Lordships are desirous that for this purpose a Manual be compiled, giving general instructions for the observation and for record in various branches of Science."[1]

The idea, therefore, was not only to aid plant collecting and botany but such subjects as zoology, astronomy, geology, geography and hydrography.

Their Lordships were not keen for officers to be too seriously involved and they considered it was not necessary "that this manual should be one of very deep and abstruse research".[1] It would be for their Lordships to consider, the Memorandum went on, suddenly producing a carrot out of a lace cuff, "whether some pecuniary reward or promotion may not be given to those who succeed in producing eminently useful results."[1]

The Commissioners saw that their book of instructions might filter down to the merchant navy with useful effect, for the Memorandum ends with that although Her Majesty had "cruisers in every sea" there were places occasionally where ships of the Navy were not present and where vessels of the merchant were and "conducted with much intelligence and enterprise wherefor the Manual would be valuable".[1]

The Handbook was to run to several editions and to have a number of distinguished editors and contributors. Sir William Hooker, Regis Professor of Botany in the University of Glasgow, for example, wrote the article on

1. Herschel, Sir John F.W., Bart., Editor, A *Manual of Scientific Inquiry* — Prepared for the use of officers in Her Majesty's Navy and Travellers in General, John Murray, London, 1849.

that subject and Charles Darwin on geology.

The book brought together, in one volume, a series of instructions that were to be found before in pamphlets kept in the chart drawer, sandwiched amongst the pilot's guides or, indeed, nestling under the medical officer's hose on many a Royal Navy ship.

The Hydrographic Office had commissioned W. Clowes of 14 Charing Cross to print Sir William Hooker's three page pamphlet *Directions for Collecting and Preserving Plants in Foreign Countries* that he had first penned in Glasgow in 1828.[2]

In this edition, the directions are divided into two. The first section is headed "Preserving Plants for a Hortus Siccus" and the second on "How to Care for Seeds and Plants for Cultivation".

By the time the fourth edition was published in 1871 the order was reversed and the chapter titles became "Living Plants for Cultivation" and "Preserving Plants for the Herbarium". It is interesting to look at the instructions for the preservation of plant life. Sir William points out in both that the easiest way to introduce plants from abroad is by the collection of perfectly ripe seed "kept dry in a box". Rooted plants, so the 1828 instructions go "should be carefully placed together, but not too crowded, with common soil, in wooden boxes, the top of which is formed with two sloping sides like the roof of a house; one of these constitutes a lid that can be opened or shut at pleasure, so as to admit the air and water, and especially so as to exclude the spray of the sea, which would be highly prejudicial. The earth must be kept moderately moist, and the boxes always placed either on an exposed part of the deck of the vessel, or slung from the tops". The author meant the platform at the head of the lower masts, creating in so doing, greenhouses in the sky. William Hooker continues that in this situation "they are liable to the least injury" though he recognises that "the person who has charge of them must not forget to supply them with fresh water when they may require it". By the time the fourth edition was published, these precautions were not necessary. Indeed, "the lid is fastened with putty and screws and the glass protected with a piece of stout wire netting or battens of wood." The case is then placed on the deck so as to be exposed to the light "which is an indispensible requisite". Sir William's son, Joseph by now editing his father's work says that plants in such a situation "will require no watering nor any attention (unless the glass happens to be broken) during the entire voyage". He warns that the case "should be made so that the bottom is raised several inches above the deck, in order that they may not be soaked with salt water when washing decks, etc.; and care should be taken to put broken potsherds in the bottom of the case before the earth is put in".

The revolution that produced this change of instruction had been brought about by Dr. Nathaniel Bagshaw Ward and his Wardian Case. Nathaniel Ward came upon his invention in 1829 after observing seedlings of grass and fern thriving in a mould in a sealed bottle containing a chrysalis of a hawk-moth. He told William Hooker all about this in a letter published in the *Companion to the Botanical Magazine* published in 1842.[3]

His invention provided a sheltered micro-climate when sunlight causes the plants to transpire, droplets condensing on the glass, dropping onto the soil at night. This continuous process enabled plants to be carried from one country to another oblivious of sharp variations in temperature and flurries

2. Hooker, William Jackson, LLD, Regis Professor of Botany in the University of Glasgow, *Directions For Collecting and Preserving Plants in Foreign Countries*, W. Clowes, London, 1828.

3. Hooker, Sir William, Editor *Companion to the Botanical Magazine*, London, 1842.

Julian Barrow, *Bramdean*, Private Collection

Stanley Spencer, *Cottages at Burghclere,*
Fitzwilliam Museum

British School, 18th. century,
Chawton House, (detail) Private Collection

of salt spray which had proved so disastrous to travelling plants in the past. The Wardian case proved not only to be of economical and botanical advantage but moved from the deck and masthead tops to decorate the Victorian drawing-room table.

The idea of committing to paper instructions on how to carry seeds and plants safely across the sea came to John Ellis and he must be considered one of the pioneers, though he had been preceded by James Woodward's *Brief Instructions for Making Observations in All Parts of the World*[4] and John Evelyn who observed that "plants" or roots that come from abroad will be better preserved if they are rubbed over with honey before they are covered with mosse".[5]

Ellis was born in Ireland in about 1710 and set up as a merchant in London. Later he became agent for West Florida and then Dominica, in the West Indies. This experience led him to write in 1770, *Directions for Bringing Over Seeds and Plants From the West Indies*. He wrote, "It might be reasonably supposed, from the quantity and variety of seeds which we yearly receive from China, that we should soon be in possession of the most valuable plants of that vast empire; yet it is certain that scare one in fifty ever comes to anything, except for a few varieties of annual plants which have been common in our gardens for many years".[6]

In 1774 and 1775 Ellis published descriptions of the coffee tree, the mangoatan and the breadfruit. It was the supposed economic advantages of the latter that led to the most famous, or perhaps infamous, plant collecting expedition in history, the voyage of the *Bounty*. Though accounts show that the wake of the *Bounty* was dogged in every way with disaster, its happening was of fundamental importance in the history of early economic plant collecting. It also brought into focus the inter-related activities of those who were playing such an important part in gathering knowledge and plants from all corners of the world, with the help of the Royal Navy, in the last half of the 18th and the first half of the 19th centuries.

Breadfruit Bligh (1754-1815) earnt his nickname. Bligh had sailed with James Cook in his second expedition around the world, 1772-1774, as sailing master of the *Resolution*. In the first circumnavigation Cook had visited Tahiti to record the transit of Venus across the face of the sun. On this expedition he was accompanied by Sir Joseph Banks (1743-1820) and Dr. Daniel Solander (1736-1782), a favourite pupil of Linnaeus. John Ellis approved of the first expedition for he wrote to Solander that "no people ever went to sea better fitted out for the purpose of natural history, nor more elegantly".[7]

While in Tahiti, Banks came across the breadfruit, *Artocarpus communis*. Amazed at the productivity of the tree he wrote:

"Scarcely can it be said that they earn their bread by the sweat of their brow, when the chiefest, breadfruit, is procured by no more trouble than that of climbing a tree and pulling it down. Not that the trees grow here spontaneously, but if a man should in the course of his lifetime, plant ten such trees, which if well done might take the labour of an hour or there abouts, he would as completely fulfill his duty to his own as well as future generations as we natives of less temperate climates can do by toiling in the cold of winter and in the heat of summer to reap the annual produce of our soil."[7]

Banks was, therefore, well qualified to mastermind in 1788 the transport

4. Woodward, James, *Brief Instructions for Making Observations in All Parts of the World*, London, 1696.

5. Evelyn, John, Letter to Samuel Pepys quoted in *The problems of Transporting Plants, The Garden* — A celebration of 1000 years of British Gardening, guide to Exhibition, Victoria & Albert Museum, 1979.

6. Ellis, John, *Directions for Bringing Seeds & Plants From the West Indies & Distant Countries In A State of Vegetation*, London, 1770.

7. Lyte, Charles, *Sir Joseph Banks*, David & Charles, Newton Abbot, 1980.

of breadfruit seedlings from Tahiti to the West Indies and so to provide an economic source of food for the slaves working in the sugar plantations.

Bligh left his anchorage in Spithead on the 23rd of December, 1787. He was later to prove a gallant and competent officer. He would serve at Copenhagen and Camperdown and eventually climb to the rank of Vice-Admiral of the Blue. He sailed with Bank's blessing, but he was not a good choice for a long voyage that was not contained by the confines or the excitements of war. He was irascible and over-bearing. Today we would say that he had a "short fuse" and it blew at the slightest overload. The destination, Tahiti, was one of the most delicious places seaward of heaven where, in the words of the Dictionary of National Biography, his crew "became demoralised by a luxurious climate and unrestricted intercourse with the natives".[8]

"Breadfruit" Bligh and hothouse life was not the only cause for the famous mutiny, for sailors are not gardeners. Joseph Banks had given proper instructions on how the young trees collected on the island were to be tended. The 1,015 seedlings were disposed down below, throughout the after part of the ship, placed in racked pots. Banks was determined that the breadfruit saplings should have both light, fresh air and that their leaves should be sponged with fresh water to remove any salt that might accumulate from their "turn" on deck. The continuous ministration to this tender cargo infuriated the crew and their first act as mutineers was to dump the lot in the sea. It was perhaps surprising that William Brown, a gardener, would associate himself with the mutineers and thus revenge on his charges. It did him little good, for he was later murdered on Pitcairn Island by the Tahitians.

David Nelson, on the other hand, the botanist who had overall responsibility for the plants, survived, being cast adrift in a small boat by the mutineers and sailing with Bligh and others 3,618 nautical miles to Timor.

Bligh, however, did not give up and with the *Providence*, to which he was appointed command in 1791, he managed to introduce the breadfruit into the West Indies. However, this tenacity did not pay off, as the fruit failed to meet with the approval of the labour force who preferred the plantain, *Musa paridisiaca*, or in other words the banana.

Bligh had seen the church spires of Portsmouth recede when the *Bounty* left Spithead in 1787. Five years later those on board the Royal Navy ship *HMS Lion* were to experience the same disappearing panorama as she sailed for the Far East with Lord Macartney's Embassy to China on board. The object of the voyage — to establish an envoy to the Imperial Court, workable trading conditions and new ports in China — ended in failure. From the botanical point of view, it was a great success,[9] particularly in Hampshire terms. Not because of Macartney but because of those who accompanied him. These three shared an enthusiasm for natural history and were, or became, close friends of Sir Joseph Banks.

Sir George Leonard Staunton was Secretary to Lord Macartney's Embassy, while his son, later Sir George Thomas Staunton, then only eleven, was a page to the Ambassador and quickly became fluent both in speaking and writing Chinese. The third member of the party was John Barrow, later Sir John, Secretary to the Admiralty and founder of the Royal Geographical Society. He had taught young George Staunton mathematics while a master at a school in Greenwich. John Barrow took a great interest in Bligh

8. *Dictionary of National Biography*, Compact Edition, Oxford University Press, London, 1975.

9. Carter, H.B., *Sir Joseph Banks and the Plant Collection From Kew Sent to Empress Catharine II of Russia 1795*, Bulletin of the British Museum, Historical Series, Vol. 4 No. 5, London, 1974 (Referring to list of Macartney Embassy plants catalogued by Jonas Dryanda).

A Wardian Case.
Royal Botanic Gardens, Kew

Dr. Nathanial Bagshaw Ward and his
Wardian Case. The Wardian Case provided a
protected and sheltered microclimate for the
transportation of plants from all parts of the
world and greatly improved their chances of
survival.
Royal Botanic Gardens, Kew

and the Mutiny on the *Bounty*. He wrote an account of it in 1831.[10] He was on board *HMS Lion* as Macartney's Comptroller.

Sir George Leonard Staunton wrote the official history of the Embassy which was published in 1797, four years before he died. In the three volumes he included much natural history with descriptions of plants and gardens. His son, too, wrote on China and rose through the ranks of the East India Company, later becoming a Member of Parliament for South Hampshire from 1832-1835 and Portsmouth from 1838-1852. Sir George Thomas Staunton created the gardens at Leigh Park. He was influenced by what he had seen at the Embassy, particularly the Imperial Garden at Jehol and at Yuan-Ming-Yuan. The lake was the great Chinese feature of his own garden. Its fort, bridge and boathouse were constructed between 1828 and 1836. In the latter year, Sir George listed the plants growing in his conservatory and counted 114 species. In the stovehouse there were plants brought in by the East India Company — *Chaemarops humilis* and *Cariota urens*. His link with Bligh was the banana, the species that had defeated the breadfruit. Sir George's *Musa paradisiaca* was rooted in his hothouse in 1828. The main house has been pulled down except for the octagonal library. The gardens are now in the care of the local authorities and are an important memorial to the great period of plant discovery and import that formed the resource from which the gardens of today were developed.[11]

There was another actor in this story who lived for a time in Hampshire. He was James Drummond, later 8th Viscount Strathallan. Fourteen years senior to George Thomas Staunton he had gone to China as a writer to the East India Company. When the Embassy returned to Canton, their mission a failure, James Drummond offered Lord Macartney and the two Staunton's the use of his house "Casa da Quinta de Camões" at Macao, which he had on lease from the Company. It was during this stay that a list of plants was made, William Alexander painted a view or two of the place, and Thomas Hickey, the portrait painter who was also in the entourage, wrote a poem in its honour. Drummond was an accomplished botanist. He had procured nearly 200 forest trees while in Manila on the business of the East India Company.

In 1811, four years after leaving China, he rented Grove Place at Nursling and recreated the garden there. He, too, was part of Bank's Hampshire "circle" and Staunton had a bust of him at Leigh Park.[12]

Portsmouth did not only receive or export plants through the Navy. The East India Company had an agent in Portsmouth and he may have helped Staunton and Drummond with their imports. Commercial nurseries were in action too, for the *Hampshire Telegraph* of the 4th April, 1803 records that:

> "Mr. Fierman begs leave to inform the Nobility and Gentry of Portsmouth and its vicinity that he has imported into this country from France, Holland, etc. a choice assortment of Flowers, Fruit Trees, Seeds, Rare Plants, etc. vis. 20 of Narcissus, 25 of Jonquils, 12 of Tarcettes, 10 of Tuber Roses of Peru, 25 of Tulips, 10 of the most rare plants ever brought into the country, 24 different species of Carnations, Pinks with rose-like leaves of very uncommon beauty and variety, 31 of Rose Trees, 101 of fine Ranunculus from Spain, 10 beautiful Ranunculus, 60 Ranunculus from the Isle of Candy, smelling like cloves, 60 Anemonies, of Pioneys, 5 species of Vines of the best quality, 94 different species of pot herbs. The whole or part to be disposed of on very reasonable terms.

10. Barrow, Sir John, (Ed. Stephen Roskill), *The Eventful History of the Mutiny and Piratical Seizure of HMS Bounty, Its Causes and Consequences*, Folio Society, London, 1976.

11. Gladwyn, Derek, *Sir George Staunton — Founder of Leigh Park Gardens*, Portsmouth City Museum Leaflet, 1984.

12. Gladwyn, Derek, Letter to author 27/1/87 quoting George Thomas Staunton Correspondence 25 July, 1849.

Above:
C.R. Cotton, *Leigh Park Lake Island*, Portsmouth City Museums

Below left:
C.R. Cotton, *Leigh Park Lake*, Portsmouth City Museums

Below right:
C.R. Cotton, *Leigh Park Flagstaff*, Portsmouth City Museums

13. *Hampshire Telegraph*, No. 142, 4th April, 1803.

His stay in this town will be four or five days. He lodges at No. 79, Broad Street on the Point".[13]

The importation of plants by ship was still quite a business. No one knew this better than Sir Joseph Banks. He had had more experience than most in both the planning and practical work. He was very demanding and none more so than when His Majesty decided to send plants to Empress Catherine II of Russia on board the small ship *Venus*. He insisted that:

"The Great Cabbin of the Ship on board which they are Embarked be wholly given up for their accommodation. . . a proper Fire Place must also be fixed in it and Fuel provided that in case of chilly nights during the passage should Render the Precaution necessary. A fire may be kept up and a Standing bed place for the Gardener Placd as near the plants as possible".[14]

However, in the end a very small ship with a great cabin only 8'4" by

69

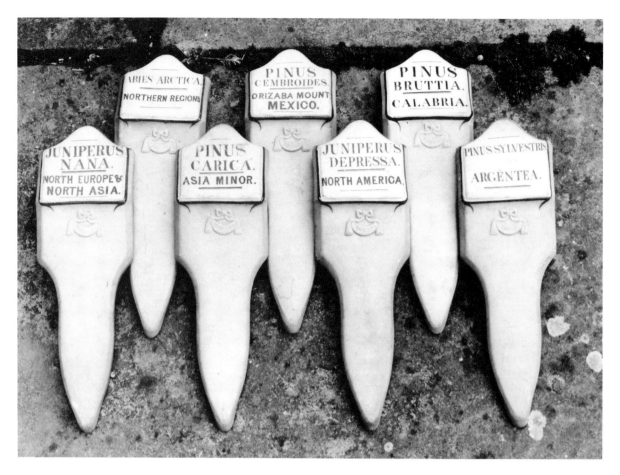

Plant labels, Private Collection

6'3" was available and so the hold — dark, dank and unsuitable — had to suffice. Banks constructed a platform large enough to contain the necessary number of plants and he gave minute instructions to George Noe, foreman of the Royal Botanic Gardens, Kew on how the plants were to be looked after on the voyage.

In a letter dated the 4th July and written from Soho Square, he ordered Noe that during the voyage:

"you are to visit the plants as often as Possible & to Spend as much time among them as you can, watering those that Require water and attending above all to the effect of the close air of the ship will produce upon them and you are Continually to remind the Captain, that as air & Light are Essential to the well being of your charge, the more the hatchways are kept open over the Platform the better Condition the Plants will be in when they arrive at their destination; in fine weather there is no doubt that all the Hatchways may be kept open for Provided their Coverings are placed to windward of them to ward off Spray of the sea and except in an actual storm it is not likely that it will under any circumstances be necessary to shut them all up at the same time".[14]

He told Noe that he could easily tell when the leaves were salted "by the taste when the tongue is applied to them". If this sad state of affairs occurred "you must as soon as possible wash them Abundantly with the Rose of your watering Pot".[14]

It is not surprising that in a letter to Sir Joseph in 1806 it is recorded that the First Mate of the plant carrying ship "does not approve of having a garden in the poop at all, he says it rocks the ship all to pieces. The Captain agreed in the same story and when the beams creak in the cuddy, they all turn to me sometimes and dam the flower pots".[15]

"Dam the flower pots" may have been a reason for mutiny on the *Bounty* and encapsulated the general view of the British tar to his duties as far as the transportation of plants was concerned before the Wardian case. But had it not been for Banks' circle, particularly Staunton of Leigh Park, the Pleasure Grounds of Hampshire would not have had the early stimulus of exotic plants which has resulted in the magnificent series of plantsmen's gardens in the County today.

It is not only the great gardens or gardeners either who have benefited, for there used to be a memorial to the Navy's efforts in the villa gardens of Britain. The monkey puzzle, *Araucaria araucana*, was brought to the back streets by Archibald Menzies (1754-1842), Surgeon-Botanist to Captain George Vancouver on the *Discovery* expedition of 1791-5. Menzies is said to have pinched some strange nuts when dining in Santiago with the Captain General of Chile, Don Ambrosio O'Higgins in 1795. On the voyage back, Menzies planted these nuts in a glazed box on the quarter deck and gave a young tree to Sir Joseph Banks at Kew on his return.

Sailors may have gladly done without gardens but gardens could not have been done without sailors.

14. Carter, H.B. (as above).
15. Desmond, Ray, *The Problems of Transporting Plants*, The Garden — A celebration of 1000 years of British Gardening, Guide to Exhibition, Victoria & Albert Museum, 1979.

Philip Brannon, *Southampton in 1856* (detail),
Southampton City Art Gallery

LITERARY GARDENERS
in Hampshire

GILL HEDLEY

For many of us the pleasure of gardens lies in passive enjoyment — visiting famous gardens, selecting from seed catalogues or reading evocative descriptions of flower beds and vegetable plots.

Hampshire has been the home of many writers whose descriptions of the landscape and specific gardens are not only of local interest but part of the national literature of gardening. Best known is Jane Austen who lived in Hampshire most of her life but detailed, evocative descriptions and commentaries survive from other periods.

Celia Fiennes started her journeys about 1685 on horseback from Newton Toney near Salisbury. Hampshire features strongly as her grandfather lived at West Tytherley and many of her relations owned property in the county, at Nursted, Southwick and Broadlands. She visited her Aunt Holt's at Nursted and wrote of the

> "drawing roome that opened into the garden, which were fine gravel walkes grass plotts and beyond it a garden of flower trees and all sorts of herbage, store of fruit, a freestone broad walke in the middle to the house; the Chambers are very good and convenient, and in the front is a place walled in, beyond is a long ground sett with rows of trees, on the right side of the house is a large grove of firrs halfe scotts, half norroway which lookes very nobly."

In Winchester she visited the close and wrote of the Dean's house:

> "the Garden is but small, there are green and gravel walks higher and lower but its all in an old fashioned form, but neatly kept and severall Curiosityes in potts of flowers and greens".

Continuing her journey through the town she comments on:

> "a good river (which) runns thro' the town at the backside the Castle stood high but there now remaines only the ruined walls and banks, on which they make gardens and hopp-yards which runnes a great length on the side of the brow of the hill that some part of the town is built on, it lookes pretty".

Next she called on some more relations, her cousin and her husband Sir John St. Barbe at Broadlands, Romsey, where:

> "the rows of trees in the avenues runns just from the road to the front of the house; you enter a Court thats wall'd in and blew iron gates, the court has a round in the middle rail'd in, designed for a Bowling Green, and the Coaches drive round it to come to the Entrance with severall stone stepps to a broad space that is railed with balls and banisters".

She takes us through the house then outside again:

> "The Gardens are walled in, some with brest walls some higher with flower potts on them, severall places with open grates to look through with stone balls or the pillars each side the Gates every way; there is a water house that by a Wheele casts up the water out of the River just by and fills the pipes to serve all the house and to fill the bases designed in the middle of the Garden with a Spout in the middle; the Gardens are not finish'd but will be very fine with large gates open to the Grounds beyond some of which are planted with trees; its a fine thing, but doubt its no very good aire, it stands in a low place near the River

the hills all round on that side and the Mold and Soyle is black and such as they cut up for peate."

Her grandfather's house, Normans Court at West Tytherley, had:

"well wooded good gardens but a very old house a fine grove of firs to the front . . . a mile thence is Basin[1] . . . the Gardens which are improved and new walls built fine fruit and vineyards a large parke to it; on the right hand about a mile off is Hackwood which is another Seate of the Duke of Boltons in a pretty parke it looks very pretty not large . . . a little further on the left hand at some distance you see a fine seate of Sir Robert Henleys it looks like a little town its so large a building and they say its a noble thing finished and furnish'd very well with good Gardens."[2]

On her way to Salisbury she visited Breamore, an Elizabethan house 'furnish'd with good tapistry'. Her tour of the house took her

"out of the drawing roome by Glass doors you enter the Garden on a terrass and that by stepps so to severall walks of gravel and grass and to the gardens are below another with low walks to give the view all at once; here was fine flowers and greene dwarfe trees and oring and lemon trees in rows with fruite and flowers at once, and some ripe, they are the first oring trees I ever saw; here are stately woods and walks."

Celia Fiennes undertook her journeys throughout England to improve her health and give her exercise; she wrote only for her family and as a record of 'the nature of the land and the Genius of the inhabitants'. Her records of 'pleasant prospects' give us a detailed view of gardens and pleasure grounds at the end of the seventeenth century when formal gardens in the French style dominated the English scene.

Nearly one hundred years later, in 1775, Jane Austen was born in the village of Steventon near Basingstoke. The Rectory in which she was born had

"one of those old fashioned gardens in which vegetables and flowers are combined, flanked and protected on the east by one of the thatched mud walls common in that country, and overshadowed by fine elms. Along the upper or southern side of this garden, ran a terrace of the finest turf, which must have been in the writer's thoughts when she described Catherine Morland's childish delight in rolling down the green slope at the back of the house.

But the chief beauty of Steventon consisted in its hedgerows. A hedgerow, in that country, does not mean a thin formal line of quickset, but an irregular border of copse-wood and timber, often wide enough to contain within it a winding footpath, or a rough cart track. Under its shelter the earliest primroses, anemones, and wild hyacinths were to be found; sometimes, the first bird's-nest; and, now and then, the unwelcome adder. Two such hedgerows radiated, as it were, from the parsonage garden. One, a continuation of the turf terrace, proceeded westward, forming the southern boundary of the home meadows; and was formed into a rustic shrubbery, with occasional seats, entitled 'the Wood Walk'."[3]

Jane wrote to her sister Cassandra:

"our improvements have advanced very well; Bank along the Elm Walk is sloped down for the reception of Thorns and Lilacs; and it is settled that the other side of the path is to continue turf'd and planted with Beech, Ash and Larch".[4]

1. Basing House.
2. Bramshill.
3. Austen-Legh, J.E., *A Memoir of Jane Austen*, 1870.
4. Johnson, W. (ed)., *Letters of Jane Austen*, 25 October 1800.

After her father's death, Jane and her mother, who had been living in Bath, moved in 1806 to Southampton to a house at 3, Castle Square of which Jane wrote "our garden is the best in town". She refers to a gravel walk bordered by sweetbriar and roses, intending to plant better varieties, and, "at my own particular desire . . . some Syringas" inspired by a favourite quotation from Cowper:

"Laburnum rich

In streaming gold; syringa Iv'ry pure."

Her plans were not merely aesthetic:

"The border under the terrace wall is clearing away to receive currants and gooseberry bushes and a spot is very proper for raspberries".[5]

In 1808, her landscape changed again with a move to Chawton, near Alton, to a cottage on the estate belonging to her brother Edward who had been adopted as heir to the Knight family of Chawton Great House. The cottage has a large garden, then part flower, part vegetable, part orchard:

"You cannot imagine — it is impossible to imagine — what nice walks we have around the orchard!!"[6]

The shrubbery had its syringa and the whole was screened from the road by a hornbeam hedge, planted by Edward Austen. In May 1811, Jane wrote to Cassandra:

"Our young piony at the foot of the fir tree has just blown and looks very handsome, and the whole of the shrubbery border will soon be gay with pinks and sweet williams, in addition to the columbines already in bloom. The syringas, too, are coming out."[7]

While she was still in Southampton, Jane had written to Cassandra, "You are recommended to bring some flower-seeds from Godmersham, particular Mignonette seed".[8] The fate of these is not reported but four years later in Chawton she writes again to her sister "some of the flower seeds are coming up very well, but your mignonette makes a very wretched appearance".

So much for the tangible gardens of Jane's life. Throughout her novels, garden scenes abound. Shrubberies in particular were important settings for privacy: "one likes to get out into a shrubbery in fine weather".[9] Her comments on the new vogue for landscape design and picturesque theory are often teasing but reflect her detailed observation of the parks, great houses and wooded landscape of Hampshire. She seems to refer to the familiar when she writes of imagined landscapes. In *Mansfield Park* the company discusses possible improvements to Sotherton Court, a large Elizabethan house. Humphry Repton is recommended as a landscape designer and we learn that his terms are five guineas a day. Mrs. Norris enthuses:

"For my part, if I had any thing within the fiftieth part of the size of Sotherton, I should be always planting and improving, for naturally I am excessively fond of it. It would be too ridiculous for me to attempt any thing where I am now, with my little half acre. It would be quite a burlesque. But if I had more room, I should take a prodigious delight in improving and planting. We did a vast deal in that way at the parsonage; we made it quite a different place from what it was when we first had it".

We recall the 'improving' undertaken at Chawton. Jane wrote to Cassandra in 1811 "I heard today that an apricot has been detected on one of the trees". Mrs. Norris, too, planted an apricot, against the stable wall:

5.   *Op. cit.*, 18 February 1807.
6.   *Op. cit.*, 29 May 1811.
7.   *Ibid.*
8.   *Op. cit.*, 20 February 1807.
9.   *Op. cit.*, 29 May 1811.

". . . a moor park, we bought it as a moor park, and it cost us — that is, it was a present from Sir Thomas, but I saw the bill and I know it cost seven shillings, and was charged as a moor park".

The Moor Park, still known as the best of English apricots, is renowned for its late flowering.

The improvements planned for Sotherton, "to give it a modern dress", were drastic:

"Repton, or any body of that sort, would certainly have the avenue at Sotherton down".

Fanny, not influenced by fashionable decrees, is unconvinced:

" 'Cut down an avenue! What a pity! Does it not make you think of Cowper? 'Ye fallen avenues, once more I mourn your fate unmerited'. "

The worldly Miss Crawford and the simple Fanny take different views:

". . . 'had I a place of my own in the country, I should be most thankful to any Mr. Repton who would undertake it, and give me as much beauty as he could for my money; and I should never look at it, till it was complete'.

'It would be delightful to me to see the progress of it all',

said Fanny.

'Ay-you have been brought up to it. It was no part of my education; and the only dose I ever had, being administered by not the first favourite in the world, has made me consider improvements in hand as the greatest of nuisances. Three years ago, the admiral, my honoured uncle, bought a cottage at Twickenham for us all to spend our summers in; and my aunt and I went down to it quite in raptures; but it being excessively pretty, it was soon found necessary to be improved; and for three months we were all dirt and confusion, without a gravel walk to step on, or a bench fit for use. I would have every thing as complete as possible in the country, shrubberies and flower gardens, and rustic seats innumerable; but it must be all done without my care'. "

John Churchill, *Hackwood*, 1938, Private Collection

The description, but not the attitude, again recalls Jane's own garden at Chawton. Jane Austen admired William Gilpin's writings on the picturesque but it is her own summary, delivered in debate between Edward and Marianne in *Sense and Sensibility* that is widely remembered. Marianne detests 'the mere jargon' surrounding the fashion for landscape design:

"Everybody pretends to feel and tries to describe with the taste and elegance of him who first defined what picturesque beauty was",

Edward responds to this sensibility with his own sense of order.

In the same novel, Mrs. Jennings commends "a nice old fashioned place":

"Quite shut in with great garden walls that are covered with the best fruit-trees in the country: and such a mulberry tree in one corner!. . . Then, there is a dovecote, some delightful stewponds, and a very pretty canal; and everything, in short, that one could wish for: and moreover it is close to the church, and only a quarter of a mile from the turnpike road, so 'tis never dull, for if you only go and sit up in an old arbour behind the house, you may see all the carriages pass along. Oh! 'tis a nice place!".

In contrast, Jane Austen goes on to describe a "modern-built house, situated on a sloping lawn". If Delaford's garden had provided opportunity for observing the world beyond the hedge, at Cleveland the spaciousness allowed Marianne to indulge herself in long walks, or "lounging round the kitchen garden". Jane Austen used landscape description to underline the emotional condition of her heroines:

"One contemporary cure for nervous disorders was to expose the sufferer to landscape that the tendency to subjectivity might be somewht corrected by a sense of those 'gentle laws'."[10]

Cleveland allowed the "indulgence of such solitary rambles" as

"It had no park, but the pleasure-grounds were tolerably extensive; and like every place of the same degree of importance it had its open shrubbery, and closer wood walk, a road of smooth gravel winding round a plantation led to the front, the lawn was dotted with timber, the house itself was under the guardianship of the fir, the mountain ash, and the acacia, and a thick screen of them altogether, interspersed with tall lombardy poplars, shut out the offices".

Finally the great house of Mr. Darcy, Pemberley, in *Pride and Prejudice* provides us with a description of a park designed in the style of Capability Brown:

"It was a large, handsome stone building, standing well on rising ground, and backed by a ridge of high woody hills, and in front, a stream of some natural importance was swelled into greater, but without artificial appearance. Its banks were neither formal nor falsely adorned. Elizabeth was delighted. She had never seen a place for which nature had done more, or where natural beauty had been so little counteracted by an awkward taste".

Although Jane Austen's imaginary gardens may be placed by her in Somerset or Derbyshire her detailed and convincing descriptions derive from her knowledge and love of the parks, estates and gardens of Hampshire. If poor, silly Catherine Morland first appears in *Northanger Abbey* as the least typical Austen heroine it is appropriate that we learn that 'indeed she had no taste for a garden'.

Jane Austen lovingly recreated gardens by description but, while she was growing up, Gilbert White was both creating a garden at his house, The Wakes, in the main street of Selborne and recording its progress. White was a curate whose family home was The Wakes. He worked in several Hampshire parishes, spending most of his time in Selborne, permanently

10. Tanner, Tony, *Introduction to Sense and Sensibility*, Penguin, 1969, p. 14.

from 1784. From the late 1740's, when he was in his twenties, he appears
to have been in charge of his father's garden and from 1751 he began his
Garden Kalendar recording the major events, plantings, weather effects,
harvesting and structural alterations in his garden.

The second half of the eighteenth century witnessed the general shift in
taste from the formal French style to a natural, irregular taste in landscape
design. White's garden at The Wakes was in the forefront of this new style
of informal and picturesque arrangement and his journal often describes the
scene in pictorial terms:

"My hedges shew beautiful lights, and shades: the yellow of the tall
maples makes a fine contrast against the green hazels', *(2 Nov 1780)*

After S.H. Grimm, *North-East View of
Selborne from the Short Lythe,*
Gilbert White Museum

In July 1776 White employed the Swiss-born watercolourist Samuel
Hieronymous Grimm to 'take some of our finest views'. Grimm drew the
scenes in and around The Wakes in as minute and delicately detailed style
as White's own prose. The *Garden Kalendar* was replaced in 1768 by White's
Naturalist's Journal with a strong emphasis on natural events. His *Natural
History of Selborne*, a series of letters, was published in 1789, four years
before his death.

The Wakes remains one of the best documented gardens of the
eighteenth century and the dominant note of White's fine English prose.
It appears that the original garden was small but added to through the
purchase of several small plots. By the 1750's it was a reversed L shape and
in the next decade it had expanded further; the *Kalendar* mentions six
sections. Two large vegetable plots, Turner's Garden and the Field Garden,
included a 'melonry' for canteloupes. Nearby were the Orchard, Quincunx
(arrangement of five fir trees) and Flower Bank:

"The prospect from my great parlor-windows to the hanger now
beautiful: the apple-trees in bloom add to the richness of the scenery!"
(May 25, 1787)

White also built an alcove on the north-western corner of Baker's Hill,
near the Flower Bank.

In the Outer Garden, White moved from garden planting to landscape design. In the style of William Kent at Stowe, he placed two large oil jars on nine feet high pedestals in the manner of classical vases. He constructed two grassy mounds, one five feet high, and created a vista by cutting through tall hedges and ranged six gates as receding images in a distant perspective which terminated in:

> "a figure of the Hesperian Hercules, painted on a board, eight feet high, on a pedestal of four feet and an half. It looks like a statue, and shows well over our out-let".

It is worth noting that in many of White's descriptions he couples the words 'picturesque' and 'amusing'. He also created a Hermitage and a zig-zag path mounting the Hanger, and decorated the route with obelisks of sandstone. This still survives. The outer garden also contained a flower garden with hollyhocks, irises, lupins and balsams, marigolds and love-in-the-mist. Roses, elders, jasmines and lilacs were also planted.

Close to the house was a small ornamental garden:

> "My garden is in high beauty, glowing with a variety of solistial flowers".
> (June 29, 1783)

The walls of the house were covered with vines, roses, figs and passion flowers and borders under the windows contained snowdrops, tulips, rockets and solomon's seal:

> "Snow-drops blow. We have in the window of the stair-case a flower-pot with seven sorts of flowers, very sweet and fragrant. (January 12, 1790)

Finally, there was the New Garden, divided into ornamental and kitchen gardens and a second new garden with six rectangular beds separated by turf paths, twelve feet wide. This had a fruit wall:

> "Planted one Roman, and one newington nectarine tree against the fruit-wall" (4 April 1786)

as well as a second ha-ha and sundial, all still visible today. The first ha-ha was one of the earliest to be built in a small private garden in this country:

> ". . . the capital stroke, the leading step to all that has followed, was . . . the destruction of walls for boundaries, and the invention of fosses — an attempt then deemed so astonishing, that the common people called them Ha! Ha's! to express their surprise at finding a sudden and unperceived check to their walk . . . I call a sunk fence the leading step for these reasons. No sooner was this simple enchantment made, than levelling, mowing, rolling followed. The contiguous ground of the park without the sunk fence was to be harmonised with the lawn within; and the garden in its turn was to be set free from its prim regularity, that it might assort with the wilder country without".[11]

White's ha-ha was built by a mason called Lang:

> "of blue rags, so massy that it is supposed to contain double the quantity of stone usual in such walls . . . it looks likely to stand a long while".

Gilbert White is probably more significant as a natural historian than a gardener. However, his descriptions of the general scene and the specific detail of the sounds and scents of his garden, the activities of his tortoise Timothy and his experiments with vegetable growing, told in a beautifully spare but evocative style, are both informative and celebratory:

> "Cucumber swells. Tortoise sleeps on . . . A nightingale sings in my outlet. Sowed sweet peas, candy-tuft, sweet alyssums".
> (April 15, 1780 - 1791)

The journalist and political writer William Cobbett farmed at Botley

11. Walpole, Horace, *The History of The Modern Taste in Gardening*, 1771-80

from 1804-17. He published *The English Gardener* in 1828, and his *Rural Rides* in 1830, most of which deal with political and agricultural economy. His journeys took him to large country estates and he notes improvements in farming but also the details of gardens, such as at Avington:

> "There are several avenues of trees which are very beautiful, and some of which give complete shelter to the kitchen garden, which has, besides, extraordinary high walls".

His own village of Botley was noted for its strawberries and it is as an expert that he records at Martyr Worthy:

> "a beautiful strawberry garden, capable of being watered by a branch of the Itchen which comes close by it. . . . Just by, on the greensward, under the shade of very fine trees, is an alcove wherein to sit to eat the strawberries, coming from the little garden just mentioned, and met by bowls of cream coming from a little milk-house, shaded by another clump a little lower down the stream. What delight! what terrestial paradise!".

From another source we learn that Cobbett:

> "thought the robinia, or false acacia, would make good hedges, because of its long thorns and power of throwing up suckers, and many people planted them, but they proved too brittle to be of much use, though some are still growing. He was a friend of Mr. Harley, who then owned Otterbourne House, and planted many curious trees there, of which two long remained — a hickory nut and a large tree in the drive. There was also an oak with enormous leaves but it was planted so near the house that it had to be moved and died in consequence".

The author in that case is Charlotte M. Yonge, the novelist, who lived all her life in Otterbourne until her death in 1901. Her *Old Woman's Outlook in a Hampshire Village* is a calendar of observations with references to her garden throughout the seasons. She records that it was "possible to gather some fourteen or fifteen garden flowers in some Januaries" and, in the next month, the losses "of ceanothus and myrtle that had gone on for years, and reached the top of the house, with leaves like tea".

She recalls the lovely cottage gardens at the turn of the century and records changes:

> "the big white lilies are looking magnificent in every cottage garden, and the little thorny scotch roses, the red china ones, and many another are creeping over the cottages, though alas! the flame coloured Austrian briar, which used to be the glory of the village is dead".

Charlotte Yonge also records the individuals who made the gardens including an amateur, the baker, whose:

> "delight was, however, in his plants. He had ingeniously contrived to glaze over the great excrescence made by his oven at the back of his cottage, and put shelves over it, and in this primitive green house he nursed geraniums and myrtles and occasionally sold an extra one".

Her comments on high summer make an interesting social comment on herbaceous borders:

> "August is the month of the greatest beauty in gardens, perhaps because the fashionable world inhabits its country houses then, and expects the borders to be full, so that more attention has been paid to the later flowers".

William Henry Hudson wrote his personal celebration of Hampshire, its landscape and wildlife, *Hampshire Days*, in 1903. He wrote it in two homes,

Opposite:

S.H. Grimm, *View of Selborne*
Houghton Library, Cambridge, Mass.

one in the New Forest and the other, lent to him, in a village between Winchester and Alresford. Of his house near Boldre he wrote:

"In front there was no lawn, but a walled plot of ground with old once ornamental trees and bushes symmetrically placed — yews, both spreading and cypress-shaped Irish yew, and tall tapering juniper and arbor vitae; it was a sort of formal garden which had long thrown off its formality. In a corner of the ground by the side of these dark plants were laurel, syringa, and lilac bushes, and among these such wildings as thorn, elder, and bramble had grown up, flourishing greatly, and making of that flowery spot a tangled thicket".

G.F. Prosser, *Rotherfield*, Private Collection

This red-brick house built in 1892 was in contrast to the little fishing cottage on the Itchen — 'this delectable spot' — where he stayed at in 1900:

"Here a small plot of ground, including the end of a lime-tree avenue, was marked out, a hedge of sweetbriar planted round it, the cottage created, and a green lawn made before it on the river side, and beds of roses planted at the back. Nothing more — no gravel walks; no startling scarlet geraniums, no lobelias, no cinerarias, no calceolarias, nor other gardeners' abominations to hurt one's eye, and make one's head ache".

Finally, Edward Thomas. In 1909 he wrote *The South Country* at a point in his life when his work was changing direction. In this long prose-poem he writes lyrically of the 'home' counties that he grew to know while living at Steep, near Petersfield, from 1906 until he went to war, and his death, in 1916. After a career as a topographical writer and critic Thomas suddenly, at the end of his life, became a poet and it is as a poet that he

Previous page:

Winston Churchill, *The Cathedral, Hackwood*, Private Collection is now remembered. His description of an archetypal village makes an appropriate end to these scenes of Hampshire pleasure grounds observed, imagined or recalled by writers who knew the county and loved its gardens:

"This farmhouse has three dormers, two rows of five shadowy windows below, and an ivied porch not quite in the centre; a modest lawn divided by a straight path; dense, well-watered borders of grey lavender, rosemary, ladslove, halberds of crimson hollyhock, infinite blending stars of Michaelmas daisy; old apple trees seeming to be pulled down almost to the grass by glossy-rinded fruit: and behind, the bended line of hills a league away, wedding the lowly meadows, the house and the trees to the large heavens and their white procession of clouds out of the south and the sea".

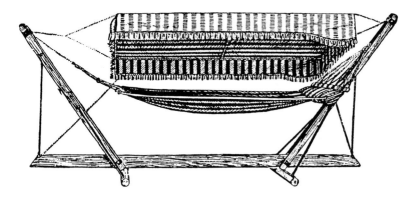

Bibliography

Further to the sources quoted in the authors' notes:

Bilikowski, Krystyna *Hampshire's Countryside Heritage, 5 : Historic Parks and Gardens,* Hampshire County Council, 1983

Pevsner, N. & Lloyd, D. *The Buildings of England : Hampshire and the Isle of Wight,* Penguin, 3rd ed., 1979

Harvey, John *Mediaeval Gardens,* Batsford, 1981

Staunton, Sir George, Bart *An Authentic Account of An Embassy,* G. Nicol, 1797

Gardens Open to the Public

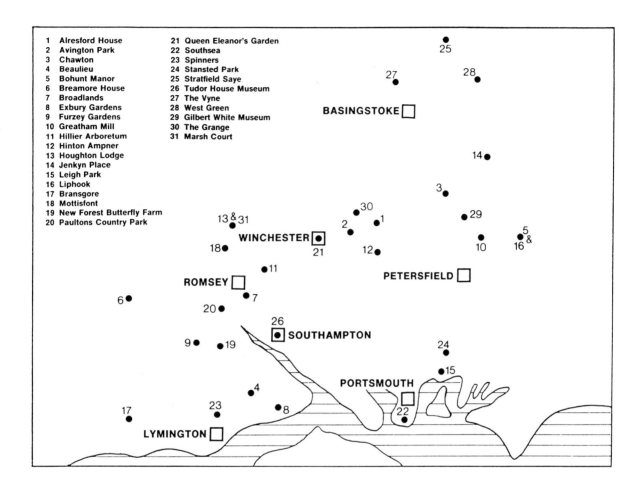

1 Alresford House
2 Avington Park
3 Chawton
4 Beaulieu
5 Bohunt Manor
6 Breamore House
7 Broadlands
8 Exbury Gardens
9 Furzey Gardens
10 Greatham Mill
11 Hillier Arboretum
12 Hinton Ampner
13 Houghton Lodge
14 Jenkyn Place
15 Leigh Park
16 Liphook
17 Bransgore
18 Mottisfont
19 New Forest Butterfly Farm
20 Paultons Country Park
21 Queen Eleanor's Garden
22 Southsea
23 Spinners
24 Stansted Park
25 Stratfield Saye
26 Tudor House Museum
27 The Vyne
28 West Green
29 Gilbert White Museum
30 The Grange
31 Marsh Court

BASINGSTOKE

WINCHESTER

ROMSEY

PETERSFIELD

SOUTHAMPTON

PORTSMOUTH

LYMINGTON

Alresford House
Alresford

Georgian country house built by Admiral Lord Rodney 1750.

Open: All August, parties at other times by arrangement. Wed to Sun 2.30pm - 6.00pm.

Admission: £1.50.

Fruit and vegetables — 'Pick Your Own' throughout the summer. Catering facilities available for parties, receptions etc. by arrangement.

Refreshments: Teas in walled garden during season.

Fine parkland.

Telephone: 096 273 2843.

Avington Park
Winchester

Red Brick house in the Wren tradition. Parkland planned in the Brown style 1765 for the Duke of Chandos. Pleasure grounds, lake, conservatory and fine ironwork.

Location: 4m NE of Winchester, just S of B3047 in Itchen Abbas.

Open: May to Sept, Sats, Suns & Bank Hols. 2.30pm - 5.30pm. Occasionally closed Sats. for wedding receptions.

Admission: £1.50. Child (under 10) 75p.

Other times for large parties by prior arrangement.

Refreshments: Tea at the House (Suns & Bank Hols only).

Telephone: 0962 78202.

Jane Austen's House
Chawton, nr Alton

House and garden containing old-fashioned plants and flowers appropriate to the late 18th century.
Open: April to Oct daily; Nov, Dec & March Wed to Sun; Jan Feb Sat & Sun 11am - 4.30pm.
Admission: 85p adults, 35p children, 75p parties.
No dogs.
Disabled access.
Telephone: (0420) 83262.

Beaulieu
Nr Lyndhurst

Beautiful garden with lots to do; National Motor Museum, Palace House; abbey ruins with medieval herb garden.
Open: all year, daily exc 25 Dec, Apr to Sep 10am - 6pm, Oct to April 10am - 5pm.
Admission: (inclusive) £4 adults, £3 OAP's, £2.50 students/children; parties £3, £2.10 and £1.70.
Disabled access.
Telephone: (0590) 612345.

Bohunt Manor
Liphook

Woodland gardens with lakeside walk, water garden, herbaceous borders and flowering shrubs, tulip tree, rare plants. Over 50 species of waterfowl and trees.
Open: all year daily, 12 noon - 6pm.
Admission: £1 adults, 10p children.
No dogs.
Disabled access.
Telephone: (0428) 722208.

Breamore House
Nr Fordingbridge

Elizabethan Manor House (1583) with fine collection of paintings, tapestries, furniture, Countryside Museum, Carriage Museum. Parkland setting. Miz Maze, Woodland walks.
Location: 3 miles N of Fordingbridge off the main Bournemouth Road (A338) 8 miles S of Salisbury.
For details of opening please telephone.
Admission: combined ticket £2.80. Child £1.40.
Reduced rates for parties & OAPs.
Other times by appointment.

Refreshments: Home made teas. Food available Albany Hotel, Fordingbridge.
Telephone: Downton (0705) 22270.

Broadlands
Romsey

Previously the home of Lord Mountbatten, built in classical Palladian style. Lovely landscaped lawns beside the River Test remain a tribute to the genius of "Capability" Brown.
Open: 1 April to 30 Sept, Tue to Sun; also Mon in Aug, Sept and Bank Holidays 10am - 5pm.
Admission: £3 adults, £1.70 children (under 12 accompanied free), £2.20 OAP's, parties; £2.50 adults; £1.40 children.
No dogs.
Disabled access.
Telephone: (0794) 516878.

Exbury Gardens
Exbury, nr Southampton

200-acre woodland garden of botanical interest, containing the Rothschild collection of rhododendrons, azaleas and camelias. 2-acre rock garden, ponds and rose garden.
Open: 7 March to 17 July, daily 1 - 5.30. April to July 10 - 5.30. 15 Sept - Oct daily 10am - 5pm.
Admission: £2 adults, £1.50 OAP's/children (under 12 free); parties £1.50.
Disabled access.
Telephone: (0703) 891203.

Furzey Gardens
Minstead, nr Lyndhurst

Lovely gardens full of variety in peaceful setting; ancient cottage and art-and-craft gallery to visit.
Open: all year, daily exc 25 & 26 Dec. 10am - 5pm or dusk.
Admission: £1.50 adults, 75p children; reductions for parties.
No dogs.
Disabled access.
Telephone: (0703) 812464.

The Grange
Northington, nr Alresford

One of the most important Neo Classical country houses in Europe, built c1809 in the form of a Greek temple round the core of a late 17th century brick mansion.
Open: Grounds all year, daily.
Admission: Free.

Telephone: (096273) 4720.

Greatham Mill
Greatham, nr Liss

Interesting garden with large variety of plants surrounding mill house, with mill stream. Plants for sale.
Open: 19 April to 30 Sept, Sun & Bank Hols 2pm - 7pm.
Admission: 50p adults, children free.
No dogs.

Telephone: (042 07) 219.

Hillier Arboretum
Ampfield, nr Romsey

The largest collection of trees and shrubs of its kind in the British Isles, planted within an attractive landscape.
Open: all year, Mon - Fri 10am - 5pm, also Sat, Sun & Bank Hols, March - 9 Nov, 1pm - 6pm.
Admission: £1 adults, children free; parties of 30+ 80p.
No dogs.
Disabled access.

Telephone: (0794) 68787.

Hinton Ampner
Bramdean, nr Alresford

House remodelled in its former Georgian style by Ralph Dutton in 1934 but in 1960 it was tragically gutted by fire. Rebuilt and refurnished with fine Regency furniture, pictures and porcelain. Set in superb countryside, the garden juxtaposes formality of design with informality of planting, producing delightful walks with magical prospects and unexpected vistas.
Open: April - Sept, incl. Garden, Wed - Sun 2pm - 6pm; House, Wed only 2pm - 6pm.

Admission: Garden, £1; House £1 extra; children half price.
No indoor photography. Parties by appointment. Teas Wed, Sat, Sun but regret no reservations. National Trust.

Telephone: (096 279) 344.

Houghton Lodge
Stockbridge

18th century "cottage orné" with fine views over Test Valley. Rare chalk cob walls surround produce garden. Extensive glasshouses and vinery, with fine displays of flowers. 18th century folly.
Open: March to end Aug, Wed & Thur 2pm - 5pm. Also Easter Sun & Mon.
Admission: £1 adults, 50p children.
No dogs.
Disabled access.

Telephone: (0264) 810502.

Jenkyn Place
Bentley

Beautifully designed garden with large collection of rare plants, roses, double herbaceous borders.
Location: In Bentley 400 yds N of cross roads (sign to Crondall). Station: Bentley 1m.
Open: Garden only Thurs - Sun 16 April - 13 Sept including Bank Hols 2pm - 6pm.
Admission: £1. Children 5 - 15 50p.
No Dogs.
Car park free.
Plants for sale.

Leigh Park Gardens
& Sir George Staunton Estate
Havant

Estate garden with lovely walks, rhododendrons, lawns and lake; large cedars and tulip tree. Picnic area; play area and farm animals.
Open: 28 March to 31 Oct daily 10am - 6pm.
Admission: 90p adults, 50p OAPs'/children, 30p parties.
No dogs.

Telephone: (0705) 834148/834770.

Liphook

Ten-acre woodland garden. Large area rhodo-dendrons and azaleas, including quarter mile azalea walk. Rare trees and shrubs. Walks with fine views. Steam engine collection.

Open: 12 April to 28 Sept, Suns & Bank Hols also 17 - 31 Aug, 12 noon - 6pm.

Admission: (approx) £1.50 adults, £1.20 children/OAP's; parties £1.50 & £1.

No dogs.

Disabled access.

Telephone: (0428) 723233.

Macpenny's
Bransgore, nr Christchurch

Large woodland garden. Nurseries with many new varieties of plants; camelias, rhododendrons, azaleas, heathers and herbaceous plants.

Open: all year, daily, Mon - Fri 8am - 5pm, Sat 9am - 5pm, Sun 2pm - 5pm.

Admission: free, charity collecting box.

Telephone: (0425) 72348.

Marsh Court
Stockbridge

A house designed by Lutyens with gardens by Gertrude Jekyll.

Open: By appointment only.

No admission charged but donations welcome.

Telephone: (0264) 810503.

Mottisfont Abbey
Mottisfont, nr Romsey

Interesting house with lovely grounds bordering river; fine lawns and trees; collection of old-fashioned roses. Garden open 29 March to end Sept, Sun to Thur. House 2pm - 6pm Wed & Sun (guided tours only), last entry 5pm.

Admission: Grounds £1.50 June & July, £1 April, May, Aug, Sept, House 30p extra; children half price.

National Trust.

No dogs.

Disabled access.

Telephone: (0794) 40757.

New Forest Butterfly Farm
Ashurst, nr Lyndhurst

Indoor tropical garden filled with exotic free-flying butterflies from all over the world. Passion flowers and shrubs. English garden with British Butterflies. Dragonfly pond. Garden centre.

Open: April - Oct daily 10am - 5pm.

Admission: £2.20 adults, £1.50 OAP's, £1.20 children; reductions for parties of 15+.

No dogs.

Disabled access.

Telephone: (042 129) 2166.

Paultons Country Park & Bird Gardens
Ower, nr Romsey

Attractive gardens with superb cedars are the setting for aviaries and ponds with many varieties of exotic birds and waterfowl. Ten-acre lake; 19th century waterwheel; Village Life Museum.

Open: 1 Jan - 1 Nov, 10am - 7pm (last entry 5pm or 1 hour before dusk).

Admission: £2.50 adults, £1.90 OAP's, £1.60 children; parties by arrangement.

No dogs.

Disabled access.

Telephone: (0703) 814442.

Queen Eleanor's Garden
The Great Hall, Winchester

Authentic re-creation of a medieval castle garden, features 1275 - 1450, on south side of the Great Hall. Fountain, tunnel arbour, turf seat, Queen's herber.

Open: every day inc Bank Hols 10am - 5pm. Nov - Feb 10am - 4pm Sats & Suns only.

Admission: free.

Telephone: (0962) 54411 ext. 569.

Seafront Gardens & Canoe Lake
Southsea, Portsmouth

One mile of parks and gardens and floral displays and colour all the year round; Castle Gardens and splendid floral clock. Canoe Lake has 2-acre rose

The Dennis Mower, Private Collection

garden with circular pergola; formal floral displays; wide views over Solent.

Open: all year, daily, dawn to dusk.

Admission: free.

Disabled access.

Telephone: (0705) 834148.

Spinners
Boldre, Lymington

Choice shrubs with primulas, blue poppies and other woodland and ground-cover plants. Rare plants for sale.

Open: 21 April to 1 Sept daily, 10am - 6pm. Nursery open all year.

Admission: 75p.

No dogs.

Telephone: (0590) 73347.

Stansted Park
Rowlands Castle, nr Havant

Home of the Earl and Countess of Bessborough. Stansted House in its magnificent forest setting, offers the visitor a walled garden, arboretum, chapel and theatre museum.

Open: 24 May to 30 Sept, Sun, Mon, Tues, 2pm - 6pm, last entry 5.30pm.

Admission: Garden £1 adults, 80p OAP's; 50p children; House & Garden £1.80 adults, £1.20 OAP's, 80p children; parties £1.20 & 60p.

No dogs.

Telephone: (0705) 412265.

Stratfield Saye House

Between Reading and Basingstoke on Berkshire/Hampshire border. Off A33. Home of the Duke of Wellington; extensive grounds include American, rose, and walled gardens, and wildfowl sanctuary. Exhibition.

Open: 1 May to 29 Sept, daily exc Fri, 11.30am - 5pm, also 18 - 20 April Sat & Sun in April.

Admission: £2.60 adults, £1.75 OAP's/disabled (Tues only). £1.30 children; parties £2.30 & £1.15.

Disabled access.

Telephone: Wellington office (0256) 882882.

Tudor House Museum Garden
Southampton

Half-timbered, 16th century house now a museum, with gardens formally laid out in Elizabethan style, featuring Tudor knot garden.
Open: all year, daily exc Mon; Tues - Fri 10am - 5pm; Sat 10am - 4pm, Sun 2pm - 5pm.
Admission: free.
No dogs.
Disabled access.
Telephone: (0703) 332513.

The Vyne
Sherborne St. John, nr Basingstoke

Extensive lawns, herbaceous borders and spectacular lake; historic mansion originally built by Henry VIII's Lord Chamberlain, William Sandys.
Open: 1 April - 19 Oct, daily exc Mon & Fri, 2pm - 6pm (last entry 5.30pm). Open Bank Hol Mon (but closed Tues following) 11am - 6pm.
Admission: 80p adults, 40p children.
National Trust.
No dogs.
Disabled access.
Telephone: (0256) 881337.

West Green House
Hartley Wintney

Small early 18th century house of great charm in a delightful garden.
Garden open April to end Sept, Wed, Thur, Sun 2pm - 6pm. Admission: £1 adults, 50p children.
National Trust.
No dogs.
Telephone: (0372) 53401.

Gilbert White Museum
Selborne, nr Alton

Garden of 18th century naturalist Gilbert White, including original ha-ha, section of his fruit wall, a wild garden, water garden, old fashioned rose garden and garden of annuals. New herb garden and new garden guide book. Reconstructed bird hide. Museum.
Open: 1 March - 31 Oct, Tue - Sun, 12 noon - 5.30pm (last entry 5pm) also Bank Hol Mon.
Admission: £1 adults, 70p OAP's, 55p children; party reduction.
No dogs exc guide dogs.
Disabled access.
Telephone: (042 050) 275.

For more information contact the
Southern Tourist Board, Town Hall Centre, Leigh Road, Eastleigh, Hampshire SO5 4DE (0703) 616027

Historic Country House Hotels

Lainston House
Sparsholt, Winchester

Beautiful 18th century house set in parkland with magnificent avenues. Hexagonal walled garden with 18th century style herb garden. Dovecote. Ruins of chapel.
Telephone: (0962) 63588.

Rhinefield House Hotel
Brockenhurst

Elaborate Victorian gardens being restored to the original 1880 design. Huge stone house commanding view across the New Forest. Stone canals, arboretum, deer on lower lawns.
Telephone: (0590) 22922.

Tylney Hall
Rotherwick, nr Hartley Wintney

Imposing house set in parkland. Fine conifers, avenues, lakes and water gardens. Terraces, garden pavilions and magnificent walled kitchen garden with unique range of kitchen garden buildings and glasshouses. Exciting restoration programme.
Telephone (0256) 724881.

Diamond Jubilee Year

1987 is a very special year as it marks the 60th Birthday of the National Gardens Scheme. When 'The Gardens Scheme' was started in 1927 there were 9 gardens open in Hampshire, 609 nationally; this year there are 124 opening in Hampshire and 2,350 in England and Wales. Three of the gardens that opened that first year in Hampshire are also open this year: Hackwood Park, Pylewell Park and Somerley.

Details of the gardens open in Hampshire can be seen in "Gardens open to the Public in England and Wales" (the Yellow Book), on sale at W.H. Smith and other bookshops. Copies of the leaflet "Hampshire Gardens" can be obtained from Mrs T.H. Faber, the Drove, West Tytherley, Salisbury, SP5 1NX. Please enclose a stamped, addressed envelope.

Funds raised under The National Gardens Scheme go towards the District Nurse Benevolent Funds, Cancer Relief Macmillan Nurse Fund, the Gardens Fund of the National Trust, The Gardeners' Charities and other nominated charities.

The National Gardens Scheme Charitable Trust

Gardens of interest open in aid of the scheme on specific dates only include;
Bramdean House, nr Alresford
Brockenhurst Park, Brockenhurst
Chantry, nr Wickham
Cheriton Cottage, nr Alresford
Chilland, Martyr Worthy
Compton End, nr Winchester
Cranbury Park, nr Otterbourne
Croylands, nr Romsey
The Dower House, Dogmersfield
Fairfield House, Hambledon
Hackwood Park, Basingstoke
Herriard Park Old Gardens, nr Basingstoke
Little Langleys, Steep
Longstock Park Gardens, nr Stockbridge
Mill Court, Alton
Pylewell Park, Lymington
Rotherfield Park, nr Alton
Somerley, Ringwood
White Windows, Longparish

The following subscribers have kindly sponsored publication of this book:

JC Armstone	Lady Bourne	Mrs PK Close-Brooks
Dr & Mrs D Ashdown	Miss Jean K Bowden	Comdr FW Collins
Sir Derek Ashe	Pamela Boxer	Miss GE Collins
Elizabeth Ashford-Russell	WHM & P Bradley	Mr & Mrs Carlo Comninos
Miss M Alexander	Sylvia Bremner	Mrs G Cone
Mrs Janet MW Allison	Dr W Brent Elliott	Kristin Cope
Heather Angel	ME Brewer	JR Cousins
RBC Applin	Rowan B Brockhurst	Elizabeth Crawley
Sue Bailey	Jocelyn Brooke	Lisa Creaye
Rosemary Jean Baird	James EH Brown	Mary Creaye
Mrs BR Balfour	Roger Brown	Col & Mrs Richard Crichton
Mrs John Balfour	Mrs ELJ Budge	Tony Cross
Denise M Baker	Gwendolen Bunce	Miss JE Crouch
Maureen Baker	Harry G Burgess	Mr NM Cuffley
Sylvia M Barnes	J Burnett-Stuart	Miss Peggy Culver
Miss B Barnett	Joan Linnell Irimy Burton	ATE Darrell-Smith
Frank & Vichy Basford	Miss E Bushrod	Mr & Mrs R Davidson
Mrs Mavis Batey	Rachel Butler	Ehrin & Nicholas Davies
AJ Batten	Mrs Rosalind Butler	Mrs AM Denny
Dr Margaret H Baylis	Viscount Camrose	Elsie Dibble
Susan J Bayly	Mr & Mrs Michael Carden	Barbara & Larry Dillner
Patrick & Anita Beasley	The Hon Mrs Carnegie	Mrs Joan Ditchfield
R Theodore Beck F.S.A.	Miss AV Carroll MBE	Mr Alfred Drummond
Miss ML Belcher	Miss D Carroll	Mr & Mrs Maldwin Drummond
Meri & Keith Benham	Mrs NJF Cartwright	Miss Muriel Dunch
JC Beswick	Mrs S Cazenove	The Hon Joane Dutton
Josephine Bevan	Mr & Mrs A Chambers	Jean East
Miss G Bevis	PGG Chappell	Kenneth East
Mark H Bicknell & Family	Mrs MS Charrington	Mr MKMF Egleston
Mrs Ann Blacoe	Mr & Mrs D Chiswell	Mrs CM Ellis
Prof BM Bland	Mrs Penelope Chitty	Brian & Alexandra Elsegood
Miss MI Bland	EM Chown	Mrs N Fabling
John Bleaden	Mrs Moyra Clearkin	Mrs Judith Fairhurst

Mrs Elizabeth Fancourt

Deirdre Le Faye

Sheila & Victor Feasey

Mrs Roger Ferrand

Mrs Basil De Ferranti

Miss Jennifer Ffennell

Dave & Carole Foote

Diana Ford

Sir Dudley Forwood Bt

Mr & Mrs Fouch

Laurence, Karen & Flora Fricker

Friends of Southampton's
  Museums and Galleries

Dr H Fuller

PHB Gardner

Agnes Garfield

John Gayler

Mr GJ George

Alice Geph

Ruth Gibbs

Mrs EM Gibbons

Nancy Burgoyne Gilbert

MJ Godwin

Elsie Goldgewicht

Mr Geof Golding

Mrs Irene Grant

Mrs Gloria M Gray

Miss JD Green

Lionel GT Green

Mrs PM Greening

Mr & Mrs S Griffiths

Mr JK Gubbins

Mrs PJ Halford

Barbara A Hall

Mrs MJ Hall-Patch

JIM Hamilton

VG Hammill

Freda M Hancock

Miss DN Hanson

Mr & Mrs D Hargreaves

Mr & Mrs BC Harman

Mr & Mrs Paul Harris

Miss JM Harries

HF Harris-Evans

Janet Harrison

EJ & EJP Hartwell

Betty Hatchard

Karen S Hately

John Hay

J Hayes

JEM Headland

Mrs B Hellier

Miss Mary Henderson

Mrs I Herbert

ES Herman

Mr Peter Hiley

DA Hinton

Victoria Hodges

Madalena S Hogg

Isobel Hollidge

Maxwell Hollyhock

Keith A Honess

Sarah Hooper

RW Hopwood

Prof F Patrick Hubbard

Mrs Amanda Hudson-Davies

Angela Hunt

Barbara & Stan Hutton

Donald Sidney Inge

Mrs Mitchell Innes

Mrs M Isherwood

Peggy & Jude James

Ian Lloyd Jameson

Michaela Jenkerson-Kenshole

Jilly & Neil Jenkinson

Mrs John Jones

Mrs MC Jordan

Mr AD Keel

Dorothea Kelburn

Mrs Eleanor M Kemp

RT Knight

Sylvia Landsberg

Mrs Phyllis Lane

Miss MD Lee

Ann Lewin

David W Lloyd

Patricia Lloyd

Mrs PJ London

Lady Lucas

Mrs BE Lucas

Marjorie Lunt

Mrs B Lythgoe

Miss AMD Lywood

Lady Macready

Mrs AT Markwick

Mrs JML Marson

Ann Martin

Mrs PH Mather

Peter Maunder

KR Mellen

Miss SM Mercer

Mrs TM Mercer

Joy Messeter

Mrs P Middleton

Sir Bernard Miller

Mrs TJ Milligan

Miss MJ Misselbrook

Mrs MJ Mitchell

Capt PB Mitford-Slade

Miss S Mollo

Mr NAD Molyneux

LJ Moody

Mrs Pam Moore

Miss AD Moorse

Mr & Mrs E Morley-Smith

Victoria Muers Raby

Alan J Munday

Clare Murley

EW McCallum

Miss M Nelson

Mr RJ Nettle

Miss BH Newman

Julian Noble

Greta R Norris

Mrs M Oliver

Mrs Ursula Ollivant

Brigadier GM Palmer

Barbara G Le Pard

Miss Denise Parrott

Mr & Mrs MJ Parry

Joan M Peachey

Mrs Barbara Peacock

Mr & Mrs CH Pearce

Miss JE Philips

Miriam Phillips

Mrs RHL Phillips

Mr & Mrs CA Pigott

Lynda & Nicholas Pine

Jean FCADG Pirie

Mrs Margaret Pirie

AE Pitcher CBE

Mary E Platt

V Pollock

Derek Poole

Mrs H Porteous

Mrs Susan Pretzlik

Sir David Price MP

Mr & Mrs RH Priestley

Elizabeth Proudman

Mrs WG Prout

Mr & Mrs K Quint

The Hon Sir Peter Ramsbotham

Mrs Mary D Ray

D Read

Mrs JS Richards

Christina Riddell

Joyce Riley

NJD Ripley Esq

FG Roberts

Major & Mrs Christopher Robinson

Keith Robinson CBE DL

Lord and Lady Romsey

Margaret P Rowe

The Royal Southampton
Horticultural Society

Helen Rudge

Miss Gill Rushton

AB Rye

Alec Samuels

Mrs Lesley Saunders

Mr & Mrs RH Sanders

CG Saunders-Davies

Mary L Saunders-Davies

Mrs KA Scallon

Sir James Scott Bt

Mrs ST Scruby

The Earl of Selborne

Dr & Mrs AK Shahani

Mrs HBC Sharp

Mrs J Sheffield

Mrs PM Sherlock

Mrs K Shuttleworth

Miss ME Siggers

Mrs J Singh Roy

IPH Skeet

Mrs M Sleeman

EE Sleep

Mrs Mairi Sloan

Betty J Smith

Mrs P Smith

Simon C Smith

Derek J Spruce

Ruth Stackard

Miss E Mary Stephens

Lenora Stephenson

Mrs AC Stocker

Mr & Mrs Eric EG Street

Kevin Stubbs

Mrs Eileen Heather Strugnell

DG Stygall

Hubert Taylor MBE

Mr & Mrs RA Telford

Lt Col & Mrs Miles Templer

Anne Elizabeth Thick

Joane I Thompson

Basil F Tite

Commander & Mrs B Tower

Sir Richard & Lady Trehane

Mr & Mrs D Tribbeck

Miss Ariane Turner Laing

Mrs DS Turner

Miss Laura Turner Laing

Philip Turner

AM Turton

The University, Southampton and
  District Gardeners Society 1911

A Unwin

Joan C Vardy

Margaret Ventham

Robert Wainwright

Mr & Mrs Peter Wake

Mrs H Wakefield

BH Wakeford

Mrs Rosamund Wallinger

Mrs Gwynne Wallis

Hugh Watson

Mr CJ Webb

Geoffrey Weighill

Stanley Weighill

Mrs Barrie Welham

Mrs M West

May L West

Mrs GM Weyndling

WI Whitaker

Thelma Whittaker

Elizabeth White

Miss Edith F Whitehead

Helen E Whiteley

Thelma Whittaker

Mr & Mrs BR Wilkins

Mrs Celia Wilkinson

Miss GD Williams

Mrs Thalia F Williams

Mr & Mrs M Wills

Glynis Wilsdon

Mrs Anne Wood

Marjorie Wood

NK Wood

Pamela & Eric Wood

KC Woodroofe

Mr & Mrs GE Wooldridge

Mr & Mrs CM Woolgar

Neville HR Yeates